THE MUSIC LIBRARY

First published in 2005 by FUEL Publishing
This revised and expanded edition published in 2016

FUEL Design & Publishing
33 Fournier Street
London E1 6QE

Designed by Murray & Sorrell FUEL
www.fuel-design.com

Scans by Happy Retouching
Printed in China

Distributed by Thames & Hudson and D.A.P.
ISBN 978-0-9931911-3-8

the music library

Conceived, compiled and written by Jonny Trunk

FUEL

Preface

It has been over a decade since the publication of *The Music Library*, our original and, dare we say, groundbreaking book looking at the art, sound and brief history of library music.

Not only was that book extraordinarily influential in terms of graphic impact, but it also brought to light obscure LPs, labels, artists and music that had, until publication, always remained very much under the normal record collecting radar.

That radar is now far more expansive because of the internet; the connected world of the geeky, enthusiastic library record collector grows by the second with facts, images, tracks, sleeves and even complete catalogues posted up, Instagrammed, YouTubed, you name it. As a result, the last ten years have seen a big jump in library music knowledge with information, lost LPs and newly discovered labels slowly rising out of obscurity and into this most peculiar and specialised of collectors' market.

Of course with all this new and multi-dimensional information comes more interest. This in turn means there are fewer library LPs to go round and so the prices for many just keep increasing. I try to keep an eye on the market and have watched it as it remains steady or spikes, but when someone paid over £1500 for a library LP on the Panda label (page 160) I realised it was the right time to revisit the old book and see where we could improve and update things.

Also, I'd started to get emails from new enthusiasts asking for copies of the first book (often referred to as 'The Bible'), which was long out of print and had started to become as expensive as some of the LPs it featured. So a new edition seemed to make perfect and obvious sense, and thankfully the remarkable Damon and Stephen at FUEL agreed.

The initial idea was a simple update, but as soon as I got stuck in I got sucked in, and spent months immersed in a web of library friends, sounds and a glut of confusing information. Unexpectedly, I also found myself fascinated this time by late 1970s and early 1980s recordings. For many collectors this is an area to be avoided, but I've found some remarkable and relevant work from distinctive labels of the period, many of which are featured in this new edition. Sadly we don't have space to include every single LP or label we've found, explored and enjoyed, so there is a page at the back with a list of other labels you may want to investigate too.

Also, while putting this new volume together, we really noticed regular artwork crossovers, especially in Italy. Graphic sleeves such as Background N.1 (page 159), Video Musica N.2 (page 128), Pinciana's Dodici Rose Rosse used by CGO, or stock shots such as the one used for The Fast Machine (page 169, Picci label) reappear on other libraries rebadged, or with different titles, fonts, colourways and sometimes even upside down. We observed artwork by Cavallaro (see New Bingo, Duse, Pony) being re-appropriated all over the place, especially within the Beat stable. It goes to show that simple economics on all levels remained very much at the heart of library music.

Unlike the first smaller edition of the book, this version has no CD. But in many cases if you Google LPs featured in the following pages, audio will often be a part of the search result. Also, I must point out that this edition would not have been possible without the patience, trust and enthusiasm of the library collectors I know well. In my opinion these few have really been pioneering in this field: many of these LPs were bought twenty years ago when very few people had any idea what they actually were or just how influential they would become. So my heartfelt thanks to them all. As a final note, I have also slightly updated my original copy from the 2005 edition. Well, we all make mistakes. Thanks for listening.

Jonny Trunk

Introduction

Source music. Mood music. Library music. A forgotten but hugely important part of our vinyl history.

Its use and purpose is simple: it is well produced economic music for film, TV, advertising and radio. Never commercially available, this music was pressed from the 1950s onwards in limited quantities and then sent directly to production houses and radio stations for use when necessary.

With any new programme, producers on a budget have limited options. To commission a new theme is expensive, so it makes economic sense to use the mood music library and instantly access a wealth of well played, potentially suitable tracks. Themes from *Mastermind*, *Grange Hill*, *Screen Test*, *On The Buses*, *Budgie*, even *Terry and June* were all well placed library music cues. And its range isn't limited to TV: George Romero, the Shaw Brothers, Gerard Damiano – all cult directors – used library music to enviable effect.

From the mid-1960s onwards, as TV and radio productions increased, so did the number of library companies across Europe. All these labels bombarded potential international users with new recordings on a regular basis. This created a competitive marketplace, where a good graphic or LP title could well make a difference in the cutting room.

With restricted budgets, peculiar 'themed' music and an unusual, invisible audience, artwork for these LPs ended up in a category all of its own, as did the music. These were the soundtracks to scenes that didn't yet exist. Add to this talented session men, tight deadlines, various new synthesisers, electronics and sonic fashions, and you had an extraordinary breeding ground for a very different sound.

The 1960s and 1970s were unique periods for music in the UK as the Musicians Union (MU), in an attempt to protect 'live' music and its members, complicated the music production system. It stated that all sessions recorded in the UK must be documented correctly and that every participating musician must be credited and paid, not only for the session but whenever a track was used. This presented libraries with a bureaucratic nightmare. The ruling negated the whole purpose of production music as a source of cheap and affordable sound. It led to a quiet but mass exodus across the Channel, to France, Belgium and Germany where countless sessions were safely recorded. London still had some output, but if suspicions were aroused and sessions were spotted as library, the notorious 'Dr. Death' from the MU would cancel the recordings immediately. By the late 1970s the MU finally realised the destructive influence of its ruling and lifted it.

Throughout the era, some of the leading jazz, classical and avant-garde musicians across Europe and America found themselves making library recordings. Many were involved just once, others (like Alan Hawkshaw) made literally thousands of usable themes and variations for Europe and beyond. It is complicated for the library collector or archivist to trace the names of the artists, as many pseudonyms were used. Lee Mason, for example, is really brassman Pete Winslow. Ipcress, a collectable Italian artist, is master soundtracker Stelvio Cipriani. Roger Roger and Nino Nardini are real names, but both also recorded under various pseudonyms. Vocal recordings in library music are rare. Barbara Moore immediately springs to mind as one of the more successful composers and vocalists in this area. Other scat or wordless vocal artists are out there too, but few real songs are to be found anywhere. An exception is the Electric Banana LPs issued by De Wolfe in the late 1960s, whose sought-after, mod-like recordings feature members of The Pretty Things.

As is evident in the pages that follow, there are and have been numerous labels and manufacturers of source music. Many of these labels are still active today, while some have been swallowed up by larger conglomerates and others have disappeared without a trace. Adding to the complication and interest in collecting are the seemingly endless lost and unique labels that have resurfaced over the last few years. Robert Vigier, Nike and Bang!! Bang!! are all examples of obscure labels with no apparent history, archive or new owners. No doubt other libraries will remain lost.

As CDs started to make their ugly way into our lives, libraries stopped producing vinyl and this large, cumbersome format was rapidly replaced. Throughout the 1980s and early 1990s much of the vinyl sitting idle in TV and radio stations was destroyed, skipped or just given away. By the mid-1990s, adventurous music collectors started to listen back. New and different sounds were being found on these old neglected LPs – weird beats, odd instrumentations, albums full of dark jazzy interludes or bizarre garage rock. Word spread about these LPs, and finding and collecting them became difficult and expensive as prices for these non-commercial pressings began to escalate. Either in clubs, through the sampler or from exotic home listening, library music was enjoying a small renaissance which continues today.

This book brings together an archive of vintage library records assembled by some of the earliest collectors. This is not a buyers' guide, or by any means a completists' catalogue. It is a visual celebration of some of the greatest unseen sleeves and unheard music ever made.

Jonny Trunk

Foreword

Pop too poppy? Rock too rocky? Funk too funky? Jazz too jazzy? Classical too classical? Avant-garde too avant-garde? Don't worry, there is an alternative… a kind of fusion of all these elements – library music. So what is it about library music?

Since the 1950s two of library music's favourite themes seem to have been those features of modern life – 'activity' and 'apprehension'. (Don't worry: there's deep sea diving and space exploration too.) The best library albums and tracks sound like some of the most modern music ever made. They have that same 'out of this world' feel which is present in all sorts of so called 'background' music. (Similar in feel, incidentally, to the hotel lift Muzak I heard while The Specials were on tour in America in 1980, which inspired me to try to incorporate it into the band's second album – a move regarded as so radical at the time it was described as 'commercial suicide'.) Library music seems to get every musical genre just slightly wrong enough to sound a bit twisted and different (i.e. great). It created a sort of super genre all of its own. Some of it is just pure... library, it doesn't sound quite like anything you've ever heard before. Library was intended to extract the 'mood' from all sorts of music, and sometimes it seems to capture the feel of an era better than the music which was actually sold at that time. If you want to find that strange ingredient which makes modern music modern, futuristic library music isn't a bad place to look.

Maybe library music's strange appeal has something to do with the musicians being heard and not seen. There are no pictures of them on the record sleeves, no personality cult, no fashion, no looks or age to confuse things. Another plus is that not a note of this music was ever played live, or sold directly to the public, so irrelevant irritations like audience reaction or 'commercial viability' weren't really a consideration. This was a sort of underworld, where the record buying public or critics wouldn't dream of venturing. To create different 'atmospheres', musicians could do whatever came into their heads, and they did, without any restrictions – apart from the fact that they had an album to make before lunch of course, not much time for self-indulgence.

Some of the musicians were well respected modern classical, film or jazz composers, probably in need of extra cash. The daughter of Italian composer Paulo Renosto says he found real creative freedom in the world of library music under the name of Lesiman, away from his struggles in the world of film and classical music (page 237). There were other great library musicians who were complete 'failures' in the 'real' music world: their only legacy is the library music they made, either for a fee, or in the hope that someone somewhere would choose their track as a soundtrack for a TV drama, science programme, radio play, B-movie or porn film. How much of their output ever actually got used is anyone's guess. Perhaps there is a note of bitterness detectable in some of this 'outsider' music, a result of the lack of recognition the musicians received. A poor composer could have put his heart and soul into what might have been billed as a 'Modern religious mass for orchestra and arp synthesiser', only to have it chopped into short sections entitled 'Octopus Approaching' or something similar. A library label boss might have decided to add a fairground waltz or a foxtrot, by a completely different artist, to some dark modern masterpiece. (We could be talking 'blue-cheese-flavoured-avant-garde-orchestral-with-a bit-of-fuzz-box-guitar-thrown-in' type dark modern masterpiece here.)

Current interest in old library music may have been started by hip hop producers looking for a breakbeat or a loop, and post-rare groovers or acid jazzers searching for that full length funky track, but there are other noises as well. Library musicians were cutting costs by using drum machines and sequencers ever since they were invented for home organs. They can probably be counted among the pioneers of that peculiar electronic European beat music which later crossed the Atlantic and became electro and techno, so there's plenty of sick stuff from the 1980s in there too. There are great library reggae tracks; for the rockists, there's everything from 1960s garage to low budget prog, maybe there's even a library punk album somewhere, in some dirty storage unit, just waiting to be discovered. (This would almost have to be the ultimate punk record.)

If the serious avant-gardists are getting into some of the abstract, ambient, experimental and electronic library music now, they have been a bit slow on the uptake – not good if you're an avant-gardist. Maybe they didn't know what to make of library music at first? Was it 'Musique Concrète' or 'Musique Tetrion Fillère'? Does it matter, as long as it sounds good? Did Delia Derbyshire for example, who made some library music (as well as 'sound effects' for the BBC and *Doctor Who*), see herself as a 'serious modern electronic composer' or not? Who cares? Her music sounds exactly the same either way. Apparently when avant-garde German electronic composer Karlheinz Stockhausen went to hear avant-jazz spaceman Sun Ra, he couldn't understand how Ra could do versions of Walt Disney songs. Ra was also supposed to be a fan of that knight of exotica, Les Baxter. Some of the more experimental library music seems like a European parallel mixture of so called 'cheesy' and 'avant-garde' elements. Library musician Gampiero Boscemi could slip quite happily from swinging Lowrey home organ melodies, to free form avant-garde 'cat walking up and down the keyboards' style (as it was known up north). Boscemi even recorded a track called *Kitty on the Moogboard*.

Many track titles in library music are great in themselves, how about: *Millstone Grit*, *Nightmare on LSD*, *Cogweb*, or *Moonlight over McAlpines* (capturing the atmosphere of a deserted building site at night)? The album title *Action Printing* (page 203) has to be the craziest description for music ever. Library sleeves normally carried descriptions of the music on each track. Do you require: 'Heavy Sliding Sounds', 'Industrial Pop Movement' or 'Medium Rock'? Maybe, thankfully, the vast majority of library records don't have any lyrics. As a punter you will have often been ordered to 'party hearty', or 'shake that booty', but have you ever actually been asked to 'touch... touch your eyebrow'? (*Magical Ring*, page 45).

Don't ever let anyone sell you a library record until you've heard it. As any library crate digger will confirm, a large proportion of the vast amount of library music made is the most indescribable dreck, and would break the mind of even the most warped library freak. Some of the music on the records I lent for this book is amazing, but I bought a few of them dirt cheap just for one track, or sound. I even bought a couple for next to nothing, just for the sleeves.

Some libraries actually used the same artwork for all their albums and took a bit of time getting it right; with other sleeves it's hard to see a connection with anything at all, let alone the music inside – a 'roadkill' in stitched canvas (*Andros*, page 193)? What has that volcano (made from crumpled silver foil and red liquorice strings) got to do with light spacey jazz funk? (*Amazing Space*, page 206). What are Chairman Mao's revolutionary workers doing with an athlete jumping over them, all neatly wrapped in a nice folder fastened with a belt (canvas, naturally – *Batterie* page 183)? Did you notice the hideous human form trapped inside the body of the wolf (*Red Kite*, page 191)? The same brief seems to have been given to the sleeve designers as to the musicians – 'zero budget and complete and utter artistic freedom to indulge in your most disturbed inner fantasies'. My favourite among the covers I lent for this book is the one where someone is being savaged by an Alsatian on a bleak mountain slope (*Carosello Musicale*, page 118). What more could you want from an album sleeve? Could it be a still from a police dog training film, meant as some sort of political comment on the Italian Fascist Party's links with the police force? I doubt it. (Although apparently Italian politicians did sometimes play library music in the background to enhance their public speeches.)

A last word of warning. Once you descend to search the dark basements of library, ordinary music may never sound quite the same again. *Dark Basements* is the title of a library track itself. There is no way out. DJs Anonymous don't have a helpline either.

Jerry Dammers
Founder of The Specials and 2 Tone

AL CAPONE

Video Music
Two LP Set. Four sides of weird synths and odd percussion.
Reverberi Brothers (JT)

HISTORY: Italian label, set up by the Reverberi brothers in 1981. OUTPUT: Just one rare release, but it was pressed as a single LP and also a double LP. Work that one out. STYLE: Four sides of dramatic and dynamic percussive cues and peculiar synth washes. MUSICIANS OF NOTE: Gian Piero and Gianfranco Reverberi. SLEEVES: Line drawings within a grid system and hand written notations.

ALTAXON

Orchester Lester Mahl / Mc Daniel Service Sound
Lester Mahl / McDaniel Service Sound
Interesting jazz things. (JT)

HISTORY: German pop / jazz music label from the mid-1970s, with small range of library releases. OUTPUT: Approximately ten library LPs made over a short period. Confusing titles and artwork make it difficult to tell standard commercial releases from library. STYLE: Hip pop, jazz, easy. MUSICIANS OF NOTE: Peter Herbolzheimer, Peter Jacques, Kenny Bird. SLEEVES: First three LPs have large coloured circle design on white background, later LPs have various combinations of the 'note and block' logo shown here. Most LPs are split between two artists.

The Kenny Bird Orchestra / Lado's Latin
Kenny Bird / Various
Surprisingly interesting jazz. (JT)

Tuscan Castle and Country Seat
Teisco
Progressive TV music for synchronisation. (JP)

HISTORY: Italian, c.1975. Started by Francesca Bini, mother of Marco Melchiori (Aka Teisco). See also Edizioni Ciclamino and Floppi Rekord. OUTPUT: One release, a documentary soundtrack issued as stock music. STYLE: Experimental, progressive, plugged-in, way out. MUSICIANS OF NOTE: Teisco. SLEEVES: Uses film stills in the style of a soundtrack album.

AMBASSADOR

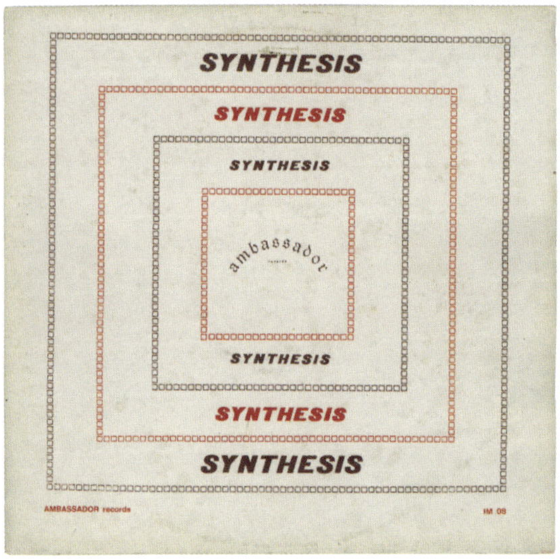

Drammi E Speranze
Bettini, Edrin
Strange moods. (JT)

Synthesis
Stefano Busa, Natali
Fairly unsuccessful electronics. (JT)

HISTORY: Small and obscure label from Italy c.1979, with possible links to Black Rock. OUTPUT: Only two LPs traced to date. Catalogue numbers indicate more. STYLE: Electronic, experimental, ambient. MUSICIANS OF NOTE: Stefano Busa. SLEEVES: Simple concentric square graphics and type. Very cheap card stock.

AMI

The Stress Newsreel
Cécil Wary
Tense newsreel cues. (JT)

HISTORY: French label started in 1971, specialising in pop, world music and chansons. OUTPUT: Just two library LPs c.1974 with AMI catalogue prefix, both under the label title *Librairie Musicale*. STYLE: Classic suspense, drama style newsreel sounds. MUSICIANS OF NOTE: Cécil Wary. SLEEVES: Graphic shapes.

AMPHONIC

London Life
Syd Dale
LP stickered with later address. (JT)

Moodsetter Pacesetter Amphonic 1000 Series
James Clarke
Includes *Wild Elephants*. (JT)

HISTORY: Founded in 1970 by composer and arranger Syd Dale. Based in Mortimer Street, London, eventually moving to Bromley, Kent. OUTPUT: Wide variety of bright compositions of approximately thirty LPs. A further eight releases on the more dramatic 1000 Series. See also Sound Stage. STYLE: Easy, classical, jazz, drama, catchy and charismatic big band sounds. MUSICIANS OF NOTE: Syd Dale, Johnny Pearson, Tony Hatch, James Clarke. SLEEVES: Generic yellow and white changing to pale blue and white in 1981. 1000 Series in dark blue and grey. FAMOUS CUES: *Pro-Celebrity Golf* and *Wish You Were Here* theme.

El Maja
The Robin Jones Seven
Latin jazz. (SS)

Denga
Robin Jones and his Quintet
More Latin jazz. (JT)

HISTORY: London based label founded by Heinz Herschmann in 1964. OUTPUT: Above average sized catalogue – well over thirty LPs produced. International releases. Strong Polish and Swiss connections. Some LPs commercially available. STYLE: Easy listening, hard percussion, scat vocals, Latin jazz, world music, big band sound. MUSICIANS OF NOTE: The Novi Singers, Polish Radio Orchestra, Robin Jones. SLEEVES: Various themed and coordinated series. The Robin Jones LPs have their own distinct look. FAMOUS CUES: Numerous test card numbers, jazz dance classics.

Melody & Rhythm Volume 1
John Fox and David Lindup
Various easy cues. (JT)

Colours in Rhythm Volume 4
Ted Nord
Jazz and easy numbers. (JT)

Contemporary Music Formation
Andrzej Kurylewicz
Jazz and avant-garde sound. (JH)

April Orchestra Lard Free Volume 15
Gilbert Artman
Heavy progressive jazz rock and electronics. (SS)

April Orchestra Caravelli Volume 16
Claude Vasori
Adventurous modern concepts. (JT)

HISTORY: A large international library issued by CBS, started in 1974, with RCA related sub label, April Orchestra Presents RCA Sound. See also RCA. OUTPUT: Many fine recordings from important composers and jazz musicians. Internationally distributed releases and pressings. Sixty-nine LPs traced for April Music, and a total of sixteen LPs issued for RCA Sound between 1976 and 1977. For April Music, compositions are by composers and played by the April Orchestra, unless the word 'présente' appears on the sleeve, in which case the music was licensed and brought in. For RCA Sound, these were simply RCA library LPs (from the SP Series), repackaged. STYLE: High-end dramatics, classical, symphonics, experimentation, electronics, rock, classical, soul, progressive ambient sounds. MUSICIANS OF NOTE: Gabriel Yared, Michel Magne, Dexter Wansal, Ward Swingle, The April Orchestra, Claude Vasori, Ennio Morricone, Gianni Marchetti, Giuliano Sorgini, Bruno Nicolai. SLEEVES: Standard font and title on each April Music release, with colour changes across all sixty-nine LPs. RCA releases all have the eccentric graphic circles, with colour changes on each volume.

April Orchestra Volume 3
Ennio Morricone
Sounds of suspense. (JH)

April Orchestra Volume 4
A. Ricardo Lucians
Tension cues. (JH)

April Orchestra Volume 5
D. I. Jarrec
Electronic, avant-garde. (JH)

April Orchestra Volume 7
Ennio Morricone
Musical suspense. (JH)

ARIETE / COSTANZA / CURCI

Musica per commenti sonori
Mario Nascimbene
Ancient and modern sounds.
Ariete label. (S)

Musica per commenti sonori
Stefano Torossi
Psychedelic jazz cues and more.
Constanza label. (JG)

Musica per tutte le ore
Nascimbene, Fava etc
Antique and ancient sounds, BBC library stickers.
Curci label. (JT)

HISTORY: Set of labels established in Milan c.1968. OUTPUT: Ariete was primarily a soundtrack label with a short run of six source music LPs issued under the title of 'Musica per commenti sonori' based on original soundtrack recordings and commissioned music. Many other LPs of specially commissioned library music (at least twenty) were issued on associated label Costanza, again all 'Musica per commenti sonori'. An earlier run of LPs were released via founding label Curci, but with 'Musica per tutte le ore' (Music for all time) as a heading, but few were made and are very illusive. Poor distribution. Some pressing inconsistencies. STYLE: Most LPs feature a broad musical cross section. Anything from easy listening to wild eastern influenced oddness. Curci LPs tend to be a little more traditional and classical. MUSICIANS OF NOTE: Franco Micalizzi, Peppino Deluca, Stefano Torossi, Sandro Brugnolini, Robert Pregadio, Mario Nascimbene. SLEEVES: Ariete and Costanza use a standard simple oval and type design with colour variations. Curci have plain sleeves with just type. All releases have complex and confusing international sleevenotes often involving full tracklistings from different releases across all three labels.

Synthetic Music
J. P. Decerf
Modern electronic larks. (JT)

Open Air
J. P. Decerf and friends
Spacey sounds. (JT)

HISTORY: Medium sized French label, started in the mid-1970s, specialising in global pop sounds. Some cross licensing with Chicago 2000. OUTPUT: Library catalogue of approximately forty LPs. STYLE: Wide range of music for all occasions, with a lean towards esoteric world music and progressive rock. Unusually, some vocal cues can be found, as well as cosmic style experiments. MUSICIANS OF NOTE: Dominique Guiot, J. P. Decerf. SLEEVES: Distinctive graphic style, full colour sleeves mixing bright graphics with circular photos and illustrations.

AYNA

Viaggio Pop No.1
Narassa (Sandro Brugnolini)
Subversive funky industrials. (S)

HISTORY: Experimental Italian music company set up by publisher Aldo Bruzzicelli in the 1970s, based in Florence. OUTPUT: Small but interesting library catalogue. Possibly over twenty LPs pressed, but hard to locate. Rare and desirable. STYLE: Experimental, progressive, electronic, dramatic. MUSICIANS OF NOTE: Egisto Macchi, Rino De Filippi. SLEEVES: Minimal approach to design. Simple graphics and titles, some repetitive abstract photography.

BACKGROUND MUSIC PUBLISHERS (BMP)

Strings Go Pop
Don Harper
Mystery and comedy with electric violin. (LV)

HISTORY: Short lived London based label, subsidiary of Joseph Weinberger, beginning in 1965. OUTPUT: Small but diverse – only a few LPs traced. *Audio Series* begins without sleeves and as 10″ records. Later 12″ LPs have printed sleeves. STYLE: Classic pop backgrounds, easy listening, some electronics. MUSICIANS OF NOTE: Don Harper. SLEEVES: Later printed sleeves have generic green and white graphic house style.

BANG!! BANG!!

Astrattismo 2
Franco Delfino
Drama, sex, small orchestra and effects. (S)

HISTORY: Independent and obscure Italian label based in Milan, c.1970. Started by composer Franco Delfino. OUTPUT: Very limited releases, confusing catalogue numbering system. Up to twenty releases, but quite illusive. STYLE: Jazz, dramatics, some experimental recordings. MUSICIANS OF NOTE: Franco Delfino, Guido Manusardi, King Zerand. SLEEVES: Some optical graphics, some plain graphics.

BEAT

L'Armonica A Bocca
Franco De Gemini
Solo spaghetti harmonica. (JT)

HISTORY: Well known Italian soundtrack label, founded by Franco De Gemini in the 1960s. See also Duse, Pentaphon, Gemini and New Bingo. OUTPUT: Large catalogue, but few library recordings exist, possibly less than ten. Many albums issued and re-badged as music for synchronisation, especially to Great Britain via the Eurobeat HQ in John Dalton Street, Manchester. STYLE: Classic spaghetti style themes, with and without beats. Often with De Gemini on harmonica. MUSICIANS OF NOTE: Alessandro Alessandroni, Franco De Gemini. SLEEVES: Both photographic and illustrative. Some identical to the Pentaphon series.

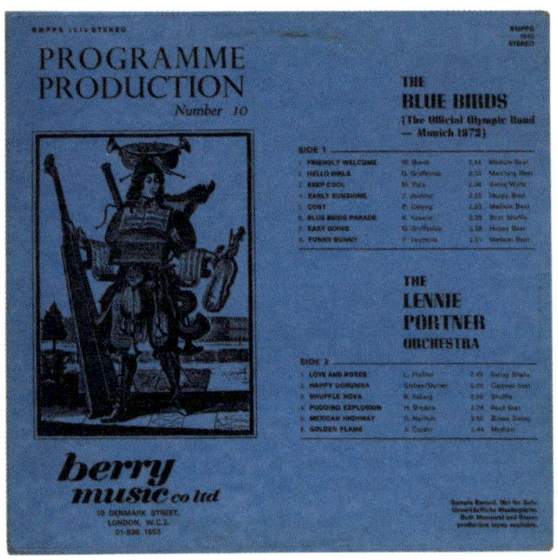

Sounds Of Now No.1
Eric Siday
Electronic signitunes. (JT)

Sounds Of Now No.2
Eric Siday
Classic electronic logos. (JT)

Sounds Of Now No.3
Paul Dunlap
Includes *Dance Of The Nuns*. (JG)

Programme Production No.10
The Blue Birds, Lennie Portner
Happy novelties and kitsch. (JT)

HISTORY: Established by Roy Berry in London, late-1950s. Now owned by KPM. OUTPUT: Large and varied, with a multitude of sub labels, such as 'Programme Production' and 'Sounds Of Now'. Some experimentation and groundbreaking records. See also Conroy (with additional links to Studio One and Blossom). STYLE: Underscores and classic early mood themes. MUSICIANS OF NOTE: Eric Siday, Paul Dunlap, Syd Dale. SLEEVES: Simple graphic and typographic styles, occasional photography on later editions. Programme Production LPs all use the 17th Century 'music man' illustration.

BIS

Sorry Puppet
The Bid-On (Raskovich)
Groovy and strange concept LP. Eurobeat publishing sticker. (JT)

HISTORY: Short lived Italian label from 1971. OUTPUT: Several pop and soundtrack singles, but only one LP made and sent out for synchronisation. Multiple copies found in the UK in TV archives, via Eurobeat in Manchester. STYLE: Twisted easy listening. MUSICIANS OF NOTE: Raskovich, aka Giuliano Sorgini. SLEEVES: Blackboard with chalk drawn by Sorgini.

BLACK ROCK RECORDS

Musica Per Sognare
Amore
Slightly questionable compositions. (JT)

HISTORY: Italian label from the 1980s, issuing rock, pop and a small run of music for library usage. Possible links with Ambassador. OUTPUT: Scarce LPs, catalogue numbers suggest up to thirty albums. STYLE: Ambient electronics, space and sport themes. MUSICIANS OF NOTE: The Galactic Group, Boneschi, Paolo Zavallone. SLEEVES: Distinct graphic style often using the same abstract artwork, re-coloured for each release.

BOOSEY & HAWKES

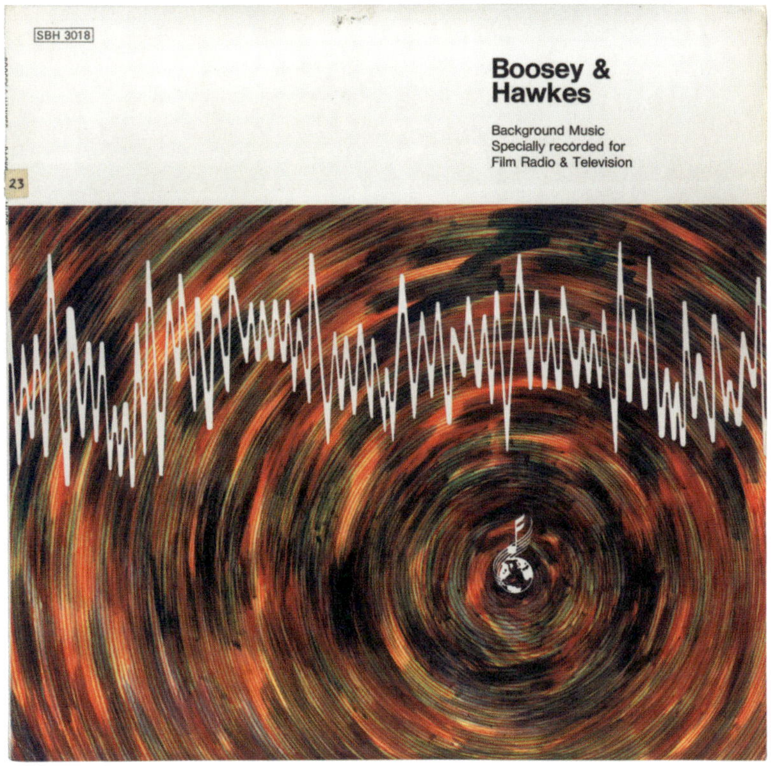

SBH 3018
Generic Boosey & Hawkes sleeve.
Multiple drama cues. (JT)

The Valley Of The Kings
Liter
Sword and sandals industrials. (JP)

HISTORY: Boosey & Co traceable to a music lending library in London, 1760. Merged with Hawkes in 1930. Vinyl based library started mid-1950s. OUTPUT: Over three hundred releases across both 10" 78rpm and 33rpm LPs. STYLE: Known for classical, symphonic music, dramatics, industrials, jazz, pop and some electronics. MUSICIANS OF NOTE: Sam Fonteyn, Trevor Duncan, Jeff Bastow, John Scott, Tod Dockstader. SLEEVES: Generic vortex and wave design. Later pressings have block colours and simple large type. FAMOUS CUES: Some *Scooby Doo* incidentals.

BOSWORTH MUSIC

Vaclav Nelhybel
Electronic music and effects.
Early 10" release. (JT)

HISTORY: London label with satellites in Berlin, New York, Brussels and Vienna. Established through sheet music production (Leipzig 1889), in London by 1892. Moved into 78rpm production during the 1930s, then to 33rpm production in 1966. OUTPUT: Over fifty releases across 10" and 12" LPs. Large number of 10" 78rpm records also produced. STYLE: Classical, light classical, jazz, easy listening, avant-garde. MUSICIANS OF NOTE: Johnny Teupen, Paolo Zavallone, Klaus Doldinger. SLEEVES: Generic blue sleeve on 10", slight changes in tone and typeface. Colour changed to yellow in late 1970s, then to photography. FAMOUS CUES: *This is Your Life* door sting.

BRIAND

Loving
Auriat, Gracy, etc
Swinging French sounds. (JK)

HISTORY: Small Paris based pop label. OUTPUT: Just one LP for library usage found in their catalogue. STYLE: Hip French sounds for love. MUSICIANS OF NOTE: Pascal Auriat. SLEEVES: Sparse but effective.

BRITISH ELECTRONIC FOUNDATION (B.E.F.)

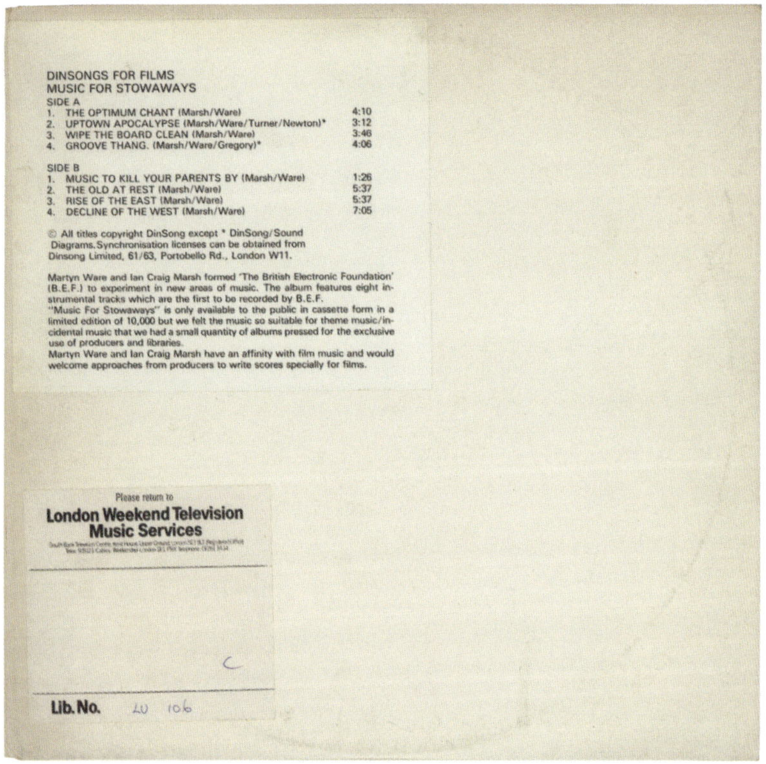

Music For Stowaways
Marsh, Ware
Early instrumental Heaven 17 issued as library. (JT)

HISTORY: Label started in 1981 by Martyn Ware and Ian Craig Marsh to experiment in new forms and areas of music. OUTPUT: Only one instrumental library album. The groundbreaking recordings (the basis for many Heaven 17 cues) were released as a cassette for the general public as 'Music For Stowaways'. A very short run of white label LPs were sent to TV production companies 'for exclusive use of producers and libraries'. Very rare. STYLE: Progressive electronic. MUSICIANS OF NOTE: Martyn Ware and Ian Craig Marsh. SLEEVES: Plain white sleeve with pasted information sheet.

BROADWAY INTERNATIONAL

Musical Fantasy No. 1
The BRF Group
Anything from perky to depressing sounds. MP2000 sticker. (JT)

HISTORY: Peculiar Italian label established in 1969 to press pop recordings. OUTPUT: Company graduated to a series of approximately twelve progressive library LPs from 1971 onwards. Some distribution through MP2000. STYLE: Jazz, interesting. MUSICIANS OF NOTE: Oscar Rocchi, Barigozzi, Boneschi and Paolo Zavallone. SLEEVES: Basic plain white sleeve with blue type.

BRULL

Bach Jazz
The Swing Bach Ensemble
All Bach to the library. (JT)

Themes In Beat
H. Thieme
Various atmospheric cues. (JG)

Synths and Saints
Kov / Warner
Side 1: Rhythm and synth adjustments.
Side 2: God. (JT)

HISTORY: London publisher and label behind C. Brull and Harmonic library labels. OUTPUT: A number of original releases as well as sublicensing, prolific re-labeling and distribution of large continental catalogues, such as PSI. Confusing catalogue numbering and lettering across releases. STYLE: Standard and contemporary mood themes. MUSICIANS OF NOTE: Gert Wilden, Hans Posegga, Trevor Duncan. SLEEVES: Simple, plain typographic style, with the occasional surprise illustration.

BRUTON

Spread Your Wings BRG Series
Martin, Dee, Hill
Includes *Bionic Coconuts*. (JT)

Wildlife BRJ Series
Kirchin, Nathan, Coleman
Fascinating British tribal tunes. (JT)

Tomorrows World BRI Series
Geoff Bastow
Tomorrow's dream, today's nightmare. (JT)

HISTORY: London label, founded in 1977 by Robin Phillips (see KPM), as part of the ATV empire. Named after Bruton Street where it was originally formed. Briefly owned by Michael Jackson, now part of Universal. OUTPUT: Impressive and quickly produced catalogue of over three hundred LPs divided into simple sub music genres (jingles, drama etc) that are both colour coded and with a simple BRA, BRB, BRC sequence. Also some unusual collaborations with Octopus, Flower and related labels, with Bruton LPs simply being placed into Italian sleeves. STYLE: Broad musical palette. MUSICIANS OF NOTE: Francis Monkman, Brian Bennett, Alan Hawkshaw, John Cameron. SLEEVES: Early sleeves all based on the twelve cube graphic system with illustration and some photography. At least one LP on coloured wax. FAMOUS CUES: Incidentals for *Space 1999*, *The Sweeney*, *Prisoner Cell Block H* and *The Krypton Factor*.

Menace BRM Series
Scott, Snell, Gray
Twenty-five musical threats. (JT)

Emergency BRK Series
John Cameron
Includes the theme to *Crimewatch*. (JT)

Electrofx Volume 1 BRI Series
James Asher
Modern electronics. (JD)

Heavy Rock BRH Contemporary Series
Various artists
Features futuristic disco. (JT)

BTW MUSIC

The Gerry Collins Trio Plus
Gerry Collins
Simple jazzy moods from 1980. (JT)

HISTORY: Small British library label set up in 1974. OUTPUT: Just eight releases in the catalogue. STYLE: Electronics, jingles, funk. MUSICIANS OF NOTE: Dave Hewson. SLEEVES: Simple blue sleeves with white type, changing fonts.

CAM

Il Prezzo Del Potere
Bacalov
Score pressed for synchronisation, early 'Tank' sleeve. (S)

Love Birds
Bruno Nicolai
Soundtrack pressed as library cues. (JT)

The Rhythm Of Life
Oscar Lindok's Orchestra
Beautiful synchronisation sounds. (JT)

Thèmes Médicaux
J. P. Decerf
Also issued on Chicago 2000. (JT)

HISTORY: Established in Rome c.1960 by the Campi Brothers, CAM stands for Creazioni Artistiche Musicali. Predominantly a soundtrack label, with many original scores repressed for synchronisation, as well as a wide spread of commissioned library music. OUTPUT: Well over two hundred releases, with library music issued across catalogues with PRE, CML, CMT and CRT prefixes. Mostly 12" LPs, with some rare 10" LPs also pressed. Some licensing from MIC. STYLE: All musical styles catered for. MUSICIANS OF NOTE: Morricone, Boneschi, Piccioni, Nicolai, Cordio, Patucchi, Decerf. SLEEVES: Most have the classic CAM logo with unpredictable changes in colour. There are also multiple pressing for some releases, with artwork changes – some early PRE labelled pressing have the word 'Tank' instead of the large CAM logo on the front, referring to the publisher of much of the music pressed. There is a series of five Mario Molino LPs with their own unique graphic artwork. Two of the CAM LPs have illustrated / photographic sleeves (CRT001 / 002). By the mid-1980s, the distinct logo design is dropped in favour of block colour and type. Nearly all LPs have multi-national sleeve notes. FAMOUS CUES: *Escalation* and *Love Birds*.

colonna
sonora
originale
tanK
PRE 8
STEREOMONIC
VIETATA LA VENDITA
tanK
musica per commenti sonori tratta dal film "IL PREZZO DEL POTERE"
musiche di Luis Enriquez Bacalov - Orchestra diretta dall'autore
Coro 4 + 4 di Nora Orlandi

MUSICA PER COMMENTI SONORI TRATTA DAL FILM «LOVE BIRDS»
Musiche di BRUNO NICOLAI
SELECTIONS FOR MUSICAL SCORES FROM THE MOTION PICTURE «LOVE BIRDS»
MUSIQUE POUR MOTIFS SONORES TIRÉE DU FILM «LOVE BIRDS»
Musiques de BRUNO NICOLAI
MUSIK FÜR TON-UNTERGRÜND AUS DEM FILM «LOVE BIRDS»
Musik von BRUNO NICOLAI
MÚSICA PARA COMENTARIOS SONOROS TOMADA DEL FILM «LOVE BIRDS»
Autor de la música BRUNO NICOLAI
PRE 3
CAM
DISCO DI SONORIZZAZIONE
SCORING RECORD
DISCO DE SONORIZACIÒN
DISQUE DE SONORISATION
BESCHALLUNGS PLATTE
DISCO DE SONORIZAÇÃO

OSCAR LINDOK'S ORCHESTRA
THE RHYTHM OF LIFE
OSCAR LINDOK'S ORCHESTER
THE RHYTHM OF LIFE
OSCAR LINDOK'S ORCHESTRA
THE RHYTHM OF LIFE
ORCHESTRE OSCAR LINDOK
THE RHYTHM OF LIFE
OSCAR LINDOK'S ORCHESTRA
THE RHYTHM OF LIFE
CrT 001
CAM
DISCO DI SONORIZZAZIONE
SCORING RECORD
DISCO DE SONORIZACIÒN
DISQUE DE SONORISATION
BESCHALLUNGS PLATTE
DISCO DE SONORIZAÇÃO

108
CmL
120
EDUCATIONAL MATERIAL
MATERIEL EDUCATIF
THEMES MEDICAUX
THEMES MEDICAUX
THEMES MEDICAUX
THEMES MEDICAUX
TEMAS MEDICOS
CAM
DISCO DI SONORIZZAZIONE
SCORING RECORD
DISCO DE SONORIZACIÒN
DISQUE DE SONORISATION
BESCHALLUNGS PLATTE
DISCO DE SONORIZAÇÃO

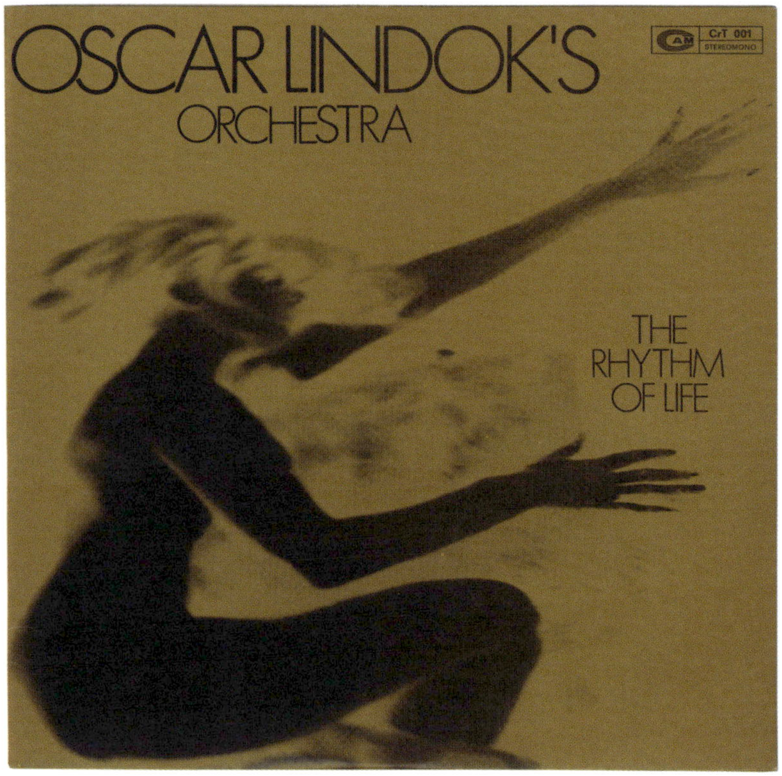

The Rhythm Of Life
Oscar Lindok's Orchestra
Rare picture sleeve edition of CRT001. (JS)

Mario Molino 5
Mario Molino
Jazz, easy, allsorts. Includes *Jumbo Suite*. (JT)

CANOPO

Zodiac
Ammedeo Tommasi
Astral-themed jazz. (JT)

HISTORY: Fine Italian label starting in 1970, with sub labels including Deneb, Flirt, Flower, Nuova Idea, Octopus. This group was then absorbed by Flipper (Flipper Srl Edizioni Musicali) in the mid-1970s. OUTPUT: Short set of interesting and progressive LPs. Around fifty LPs made, rare and desirable. STYLE: Classic Italian library ideas – jazz, experimental, easy listening, difficult listening. MUSICIANS OF NOTE: Alessandro Alessandroni, Umberto Santucci, Stefano Torrosi, Fabio Frizzi. SLEEVES: Early releases have the scorpion and are sequentially numbered, later albums use simple graphics.

Communciation-Computers-Space Age Science Release Set No.1, LP7
No artist credited
Ten cues of panic and the unknown. (JT)

Bossa Nova / Rock Themes Release Set No.2, LP2
No artist credited
From Latin beads to flower power beats. (JT)

HISTORY: Established c.1970 as part of the giant Capitol Records label. OUTPUT: Vast catalogue across at least fifteen Media Music series (ten LPs per series) as well as the earlier sprawling Hi 'Q' series. A later series simply called 'Media Music The Professional' runs to over fifty LPs. STYLE: Jazz, rock, electronics etc. Standard library thematics. Mostly short cues. MUSICIANS OF NOTE: Ole Georg, Roger Webb, Alex Simone. SLEEVES: Generic tower image, with simple reverse grid. Colour variations for each series. Later 'Professional' series have simple non-illustrative grey sleeves with black, white and red typography.

Beat Music Release Set No.3, LP7
No artist credited
Rocky boots and gas in the alley. (JT)

Up Up and Go Girls Release Set No.6, LP1
Produced by Ole Georg
Vocal scat tracks. (JT)

Bass Patterns Release Set No.7, LP4
Produced by Ole Georg
Various jazz forms. (JD)

CAROSELLO

Feelings
Stefano Torrosi under a pseudonym
Progressive easy and funky jazz.
Later issued on Conroy Eurobeat. (JG)

HISTORY: Milan based rock and pop label established mid-1960s. OUTPUT: A few catalogue recordings sublicensed to labels such as Conroy and Costanza. STYLE: Jazz, easy, filmic. MUSICIANS OF NOTE: Pino Donnagio, Stefano Torrosi. SLEEVES: Photography.

CAVENDISH

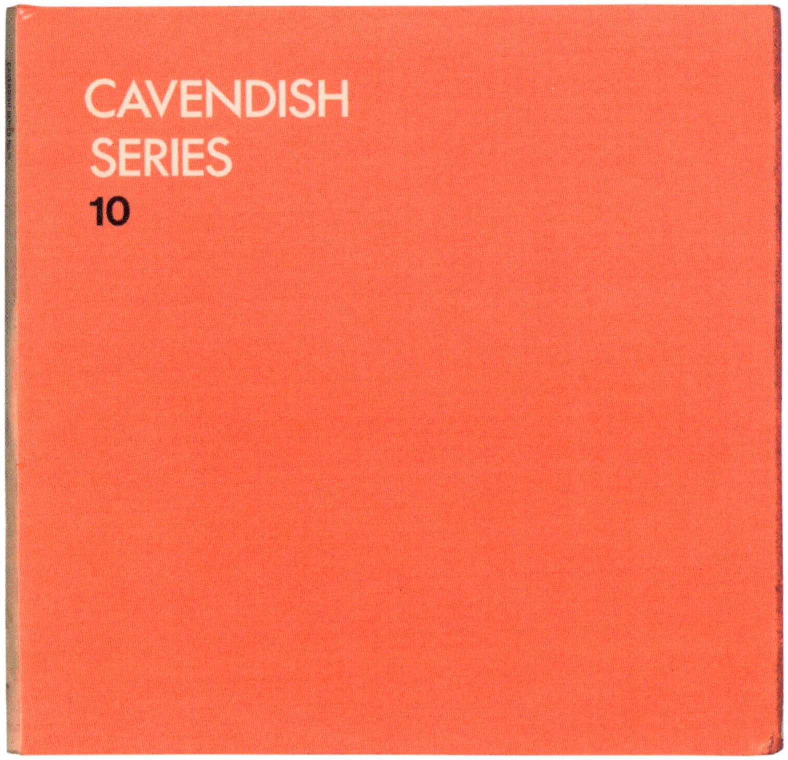

Cavendish Series 10
Various artists. Vocal recording.
Rare and unusual three sided, double LP. (JT)

HISTORY: Based in Regent Street, London c.1967. A small subsidiary label to Boosey & Hawkes. OUTPUT: Small, with eight LPs across the 1970s, with a similar sized output in the 1980s. STYLE: Simple themes and dramatics, easy, some vocals. MUSICIANS OF NOTE: Harry Stoneham, Syd Dale, Ray Davies. SLEEVES: First series plain red / pink sleeves. Second series red / orange / white with grid and coloured vinyl. FAMOUS CUES: Theme to *Ricochet*.

CEC MUSIQUE

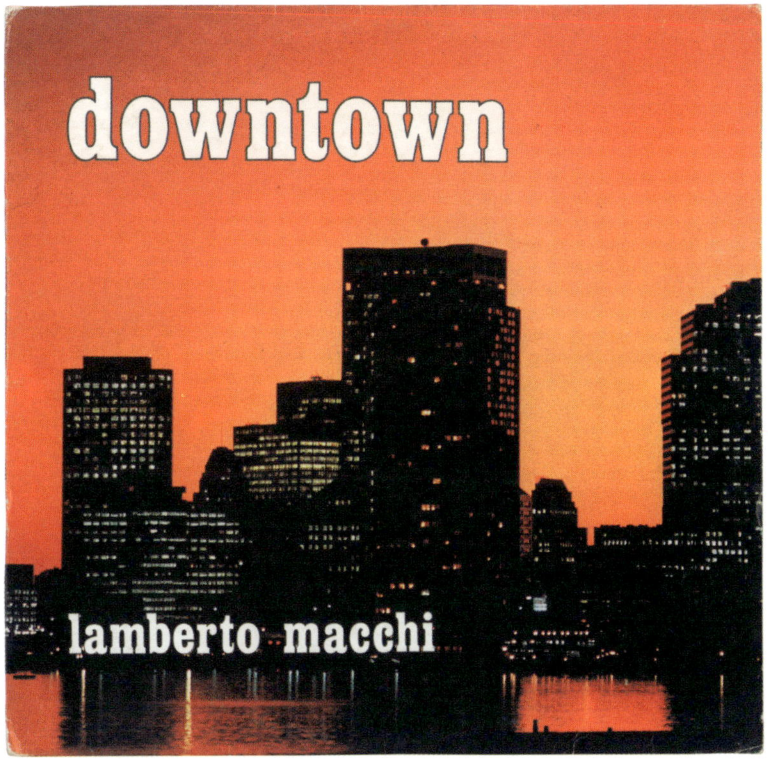

Downtown
Lamberto Macchi
Progressive urban sounds. (JD)

HISTORY: Paris based label, c.1975. OUTPUT: Quite small. Limited European distribution. STYLE: Standard dramatic sounds, some modern instrumentation. SLEEVES: Stock photography and type.

CENACOLO

Il Mondo Dei Giovani Volume 4
Max Rocci and his friends
Light jazz. (I)

HISTORY: Rome based, mid to late 1970s. Started by Italian jazz legend Umberto Santucci. OUTPUT: Small to medium sized output, at least thirty LPs traced across two series. Some possible links to Nereide, and some sublicensing to Orly. STYLE: Mainly jazz based recordings. MUSICIANS OF NOTE: Amedeo Tomassi, Marco Di Marco, Joel Vandroogenbroeck. SLEEVES: Some sleeves with 'art' covers, others with plain typographic sleeves, bizarre graphics and occasional art by Santucci.

Percussioni ed Effetti
Leonardo Marletta
Treated percussion. (JD)

Humour Per Grandi E Piccini
Giovanni Ferroni
Electronic children's music. (S)

CGO

REBUS N.2
Complesso I Panamera
From drama to Italian shakes. (S)

HISTORY: Milan based label, started in the mid 1960s as a pop based outfit, which got gradually more experimental. OUTPUT: Few library LPs manufactured, at least two found. Some rare catalogue LPs (such as Crisi) re-badged and sent to the UK for synchronisation purposes. STYLE: Easy, progressive, interesting. MUSICIANS OF NOTE: Bonfanti. SLEEVES: Spin paintings without text on the front.

CHAMPION

Via Col Tempo
Renato Serio
Hip Italian / American vibes. (S)

HISTORY: Super obscure Italian label from 1973. OUTPUT: We have found two LPs. There may be others, catalogue numbers would suggest at least three, but that means nothing. STYLE: Modern, progressive. MUSICIANS OF NOTE: Renato Serio, Claudio Gizzi. SLEEVES: A paint splash with no type on the front, an identical sleeve has been found on the Picci label.

CHAPPELL

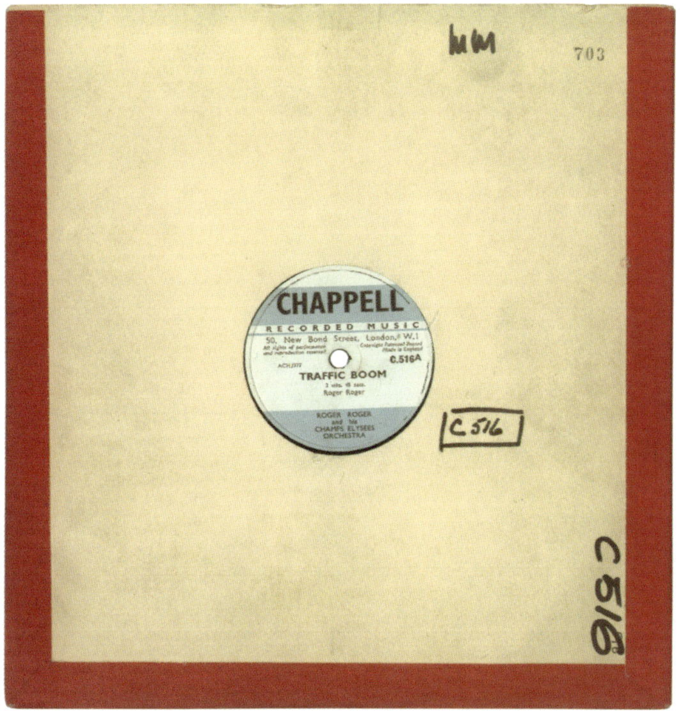

Traffic Boom
Roger Roger
Champs-Elysées jazz. (JP)

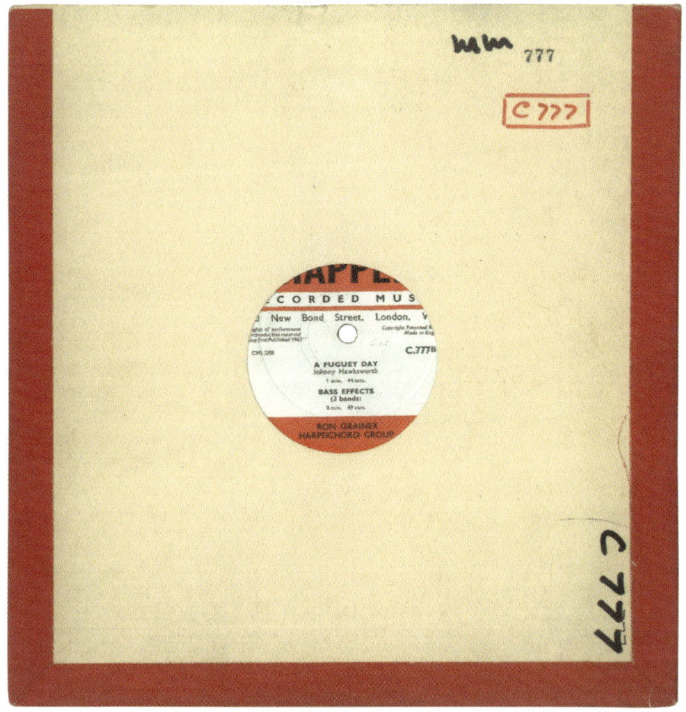

A Fuguey Day / Bass Effects
Ron Grainer
Industrial harpsichord. (JP)

HISTORY: This label started in 1811 with sheet music publishing in London. Source music recordings began in 1941. Overseas offices established early 1960s. OUTPUT: A vast international output with several large catalogues including hundreds of 78rpm releases, hundreds of 33rpms on 10", later 12" LP releases including the *LPC Series* (over one hundred and fifty LPs of both 78rpm represses and new material from LPC 1026 onwards), *Mood Music* (twenty-six LPs), *Dance And Mood Music* (twenty-one LPs), *Telecineradio Series* (nineteen LPs), *Index Series* of back catalogue and new music (fifty-five LPs), the *International Series* from Chappell Germany (seventeen LPs), *CHA Series* (thirteen LPs), *CHAP Series* (twenty-eight LPs), *Atmosphere AV Series* (twenty-seven LPs) as well as other small compilation based series. And these are just the ones we know about. Possibly the largest of all library catalogues. See also TVMusic. STYLE: All genres catered for. MUSICIANS OF NOTE: John Barry, Ennio Morricone, Nino Nardini, Roger Roger, Johnny Hawksworth, Mark Duval, Jean-Claude Petit, Jack Arel, Jacky Giordano. Some pseudonyms. SLEEVES: 78rpm and 10" records in plain card 'disco bags', repressed later on the classic yellow *LPC Series*. *Index Series* have a simple circle with red, black and white. *Dance And Mood Music*, *Mood Music* and *TCR* series have similar two colour typographic sleeves with changes in colourway for every release, the two final releases have the 'dice' sleeve. *International Series* are blue with a white circle, French *CHA Series* have overlapping multicoloured Chappell "C" design. *CAL* International have blue sleeves with white circle, 1980s *CHAP* (in red) and *Atmosphere AV Series* (in blue) have graphic spines so the complete set displays the name of the catalogue.

Dance and Mood Music Volume 13
Jack Arel and Pierre Dutour
Concept rock meets pop. (JT)

LPC 1045
Lee Mason
Includes *Shady Blues*. (JT)

Music For Drama Volume 1
Various artists
CIS Compilation Series. (JT)

Music For Drama (CAL Series)
Heinz Funk
Interesting and effective drama cues. (JT)

Pop Sounds / Mad Dog LPC Series
David Holland
Various pop cues. (JT)

Electronic Music / Synthesizer Effects LPC Series
The Allsorts / The Machines
Fine electronic and synthesiser cues. (JM)

Brass and Rhythms LPC Series
Mark Duval and his Music
Includes *The Loner*. (JT)

Music by Lee Mason LPC Series
Pete Moore (pseudonym)
Jazz and scat. (JT)

Mood Music Volume 26 CMM Series
Rene Costy
Jazz. Rare French 'dice' sleeve. (JG)

Industrial CHAP Series
Rhodos
Conceptual music. Late 1970s. (JD)

'A Ecouter' French CHA Series
Richard Demaria
Synthesiser and percussion. (LV)

Wild Side Late LPC Series
John Cacavas
Urban themes by cult film composer. (SS)

Space Résonances
World Trade Center sleeve.
Licensed to Music Media. (JD)

Dreaming In The Sky
Alan Feanch
Ambient soundscapes. (JT)

HISTORY: Medium sized 1970s pop based label with adventurous library offshoot. OUTPUT: Approximately twenty LPs pressed under the *Flash Résonance Series*, a few other sporadic releases. STYLE: Ambient, electronic, jazz. MUSICIANS OF NOTE: Cecil Wary, Guy Boyer. SLEEVES: Stock photography.

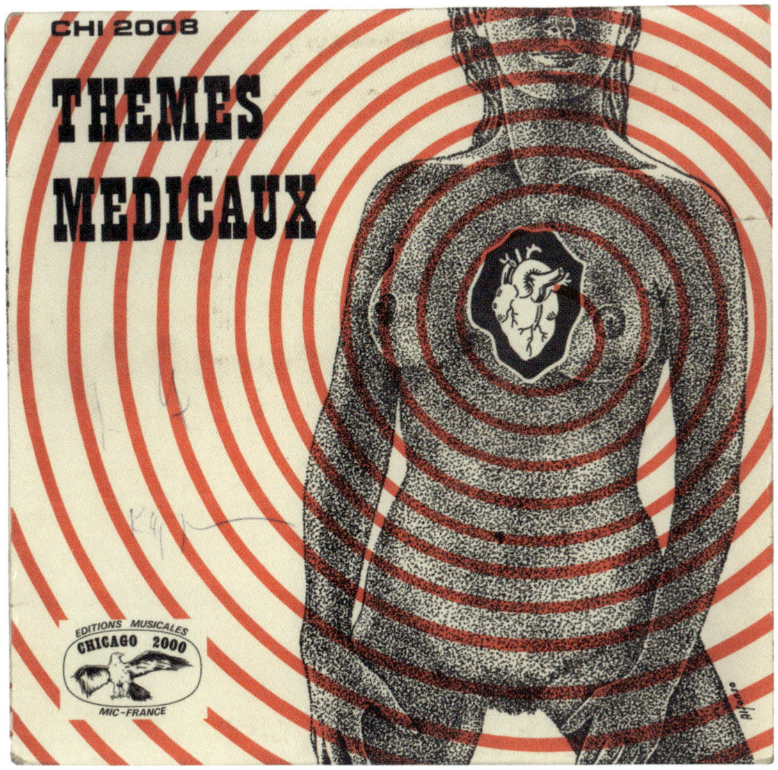

Thèmes Médicaux
William Gum-Boot
Experimental and progressive. (JD)

Magical Ring
J. P. Decerf
Unique rock and vocal sounds. (JD)

HISTORY: Editions Musicales Chicago 2000, established in Paris c.1972. Independent. See also MIC and Auvidis. OUTPUT: Approximately twenty LPs, with some sublicensing. STYLE: Jazz, pop, experimental rock. SLEEVES: The AV Series have a simple square and circle graphic device (see Auvidis), CHI Series have with block colours and bold black illustrations, others with eye catching experimental art.

CINESOUND CLUB

CNS/T301 **Brani Per Scene Statiche**
Conrado, Tommasi, Luciani, Tamponi etc
Intriguing instrumentals on 7". (JP)

HISTORY: Bizarre Italian library project from the late 1960s involving international library masters. Many cues taken from other libraries in the large Flipper group. OUTPUT: Just four 7" records pressed, all at 33rpm. Very rare. STYLE: Experimental, space themes, various industrials, heavy dramatics. MUSICIANS OF NOTE: Raskovich, Franco Tamponi, Joel Vandroogenbroeck, Janko Nilovic, Alessandro Alessandroni, Pat Prilly, Gerardo Iacoucci. SLEEVES: Identical dark pink 7" sleeves with white logo and black text.

CINEVOX

Religioni Volume 1
Romolo Grano
Diverse sounds for the church. (JT)

HISTORY: Important Italian soundtrack label set up in the early 1960s by composer Cesare Andrea Bixio. OUTPUT: Short run of scores and themes issued in the mid-1970s as library music with SON catalogue numbers, followed by a handful of releases in the 1980s with ES catalogue system. Approximately twenty LPs issued for synchronisation. Rare. STYLE: Classic Italian film music, pastoral, dynamic, religious, odd. MUSICIANS OF NOTE: Ennio Morricone, Oscar Lindok, Romolo Grano. SLEEVES: Red and white sleeves with large Cinevox logo and illustration (for SON releases), later pressings (ES) have film projector sleeves.

Terzo Mondo
Sandro Brugnolini
Futuristic musical ideas. (S)

HISTORY: Library label started by jazz composer and arranger Amedeo Tommasi. OUTPUT: At least two library LPs made in the 1970s. Very rare indeed. STYLE: Global sounds. MUSICIANS OF NOTE: Sandro Brugnolini under a pseudonym. SLEEVES: Graph paper graphics.

Fly Me To The Sun
Andre Mikola and Andrzej Marko
Contemporary group sounds - nature and industry.
Artwork by Waltraud Greffenius. (JD)

Input Output
Various musicians including Marek Bilinski
Research, production and success themes.
Artwork by Waltraud Greffenius. (JD)

HISTORY: Large and successful German label established in Munich in 1979 by jazz composer and arranger Gunther Greffenius. OUTPUT: Over eighty releases. Some sublicensing and co-distribution. STYLE: Modern sounds based on contemporary ideas and technology. MUSICIANS OF NOTE: Joel Vandroogenbroeck (of Brainticket), Alessandroni, Klaus Weiss, Eric Vann. SLEEVES: Silver sleeves with often bizarre colour illustration and type. All spines have multicoloured stripes.

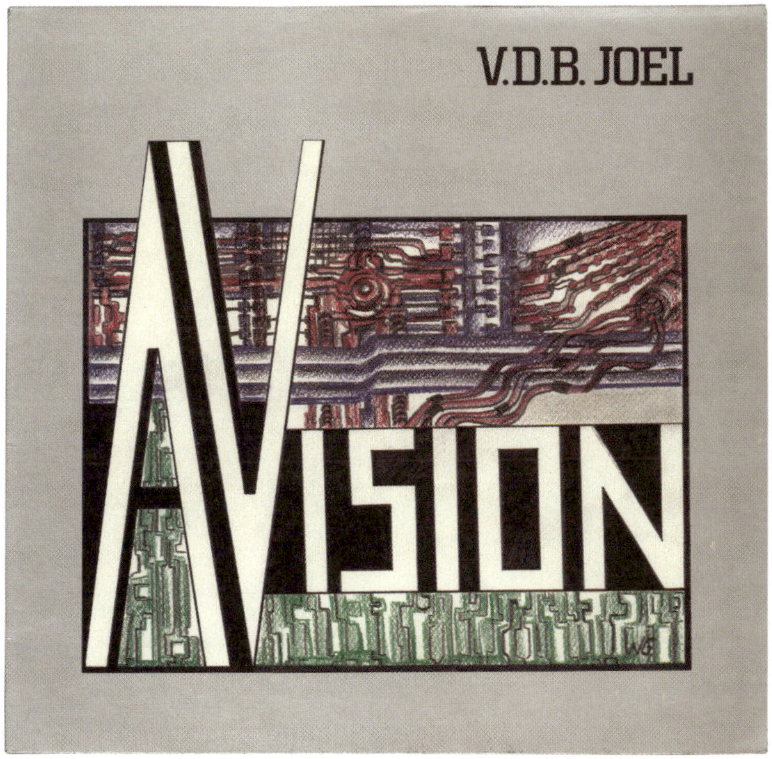

A Vision
Joel Vandroogenbroek
Science and synthesisers. (JT)

Biomechanoïd
Joel Vandroogenbroek
Conceptual, futuristic electronics.
Artwork by H. R. Giger.
Warner Music sublicense sticker. (JT)

Water World
Eric Vann
Abstract sub aquatics. (JT)
Warner Music sublicense sticker. (JT)

Romantic Backgrounds
Conroy Eurobeat Series
A. Alessandroni wordless vocal cues. (JT)

Feelings
Richford / Stefan
A classic dramatic adventure. Licensed from Carosello. (JT)

HISTORY: Established in 1958. OUTPUT: Extensive catalogue of one hundred and eighty albums, starting on 10″ 78rpm, moving onto 10″ 33 rpm LPs by 1965, and full 12″ LPs by 1970. Licensing from libraries such as SR for the eleven LP *Eurobeat Series*. Some further European collaborations with Eddie Warner's IM label and Carosello. See also Berry. STYLE: Wide ranging, some electronics, slightly exotic productions. MUSICIANS OF NOTE: Larry Robbins, Sam Sklair, Klaus Weiss, Stefano Torrosi, Bruno Nicolai, Bruno De Filippi. SLEEVES: 78rpms have simple card 'disco bags'. Some early 10″ 33rpm sleeves have generic Conroy / IM sleeves. Early 12″ LP sleeves have the record design, followed by the orange CON ROY sleeves, and then later orange op art design. *Eurobeat Series* in blue.

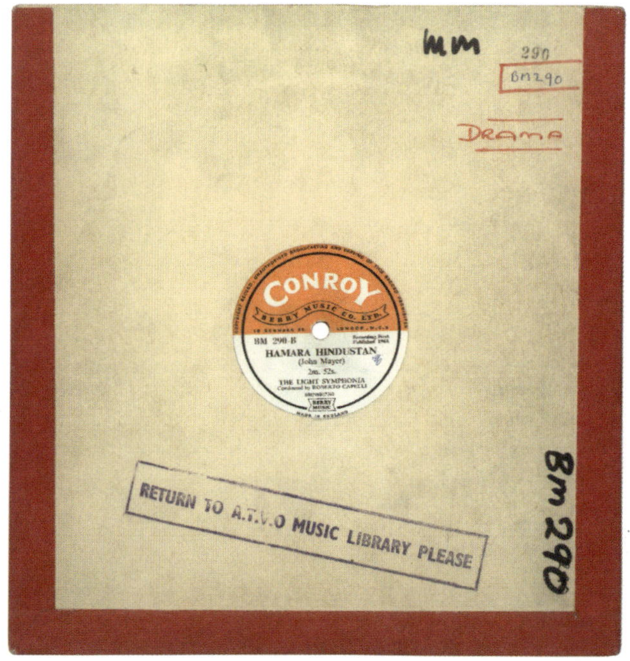

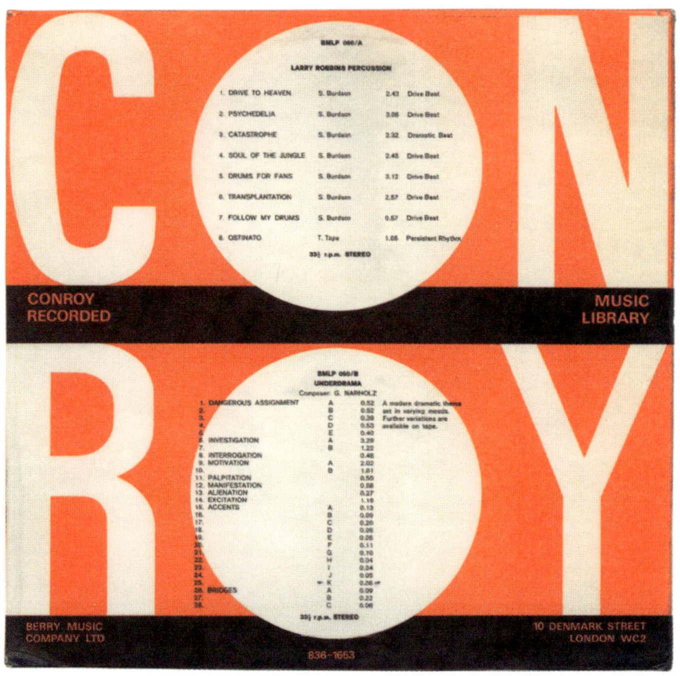

Elektronic Percussion Points '70
Rolf Quenzel
Thirty useful cues. (JT)

Larry Robbins Percussion / Underdrama
S. Burdson and G. Narholz
Standard 1970 Conroy sleeve. (JT)

Hamara Hindustan
John Mayer
Eastern excitement. (JP)

London's Underground
L. Paul-Phillips
Hard rock, said to include Dave Brock from Hawkwind, 1972. (C)

CONTACT

Thanks for Listening Series 3
Fritz Maldener
Jazz and slight psychedelia. (I)

HISTORY: Small independent German label. Little traceable history. OUTPUT: Only three LPs traced to date. Some distribution by Berry Music in the UK. Rare. STYLE: Jazz and mood based, easy. MUSICIANS OF NOTE: Fritz Maldener, Perry London. SLEEVES: Simple and repetitive two colour graphic design.

COOPER RECORDS

Jazz At Meridiana
Quintetto Di Angelo Baroncini
Incredible jazz moods. (JT)

HISTORY: Prescient Italian label of the mid-1960s. Currently part of the Leonardi stable. OUTPUT: Few LPs traced and documented, but catalogue numbers would suggest at least thirty LPs may have been issued. STYLE: Early electronics, concrete, lively jazz, some traditional music, and world music ideas. MUSICIANS OF NOTE: Antonio Luciani, Pietro Grossi. SLEEVES: Simple typographic layout with changes in colour and font.

Elettrogreca
Pietro Grossi
Important electronic noise. (JT)

1 Musica per Televisione, Radio, Produzioni Publicitarie, Films
Paolo Ferra
Various mood cues for action and drama. (S)

HISTORY: Tiny commercial Italian label set up in 1971. OUTPUT: Appears to have issued at least three LPs for library usage. STYLE: A mixture of easy, dramatic and pastoral cues. MUSICIANS OF NOTE: Paolo Ferrara. SLEEVES: Collage, illustration.

CREA MUSIC

Patterns
Peter Patzer
Contemporary electronic moods. (JT)

HISTORY: German label from the early 1980s. OUTPUT: Small output over a short period. Less than ten LPs pressed. STYLE: Ambient, electronic, cosmic. MUSICIANS OF NOTE: All LPs by Peter Patzer. SLEEVES: Economic, with identical geometric red, white and blue sleeves with black title changes. LPs pressed on white vinyl.

CREA SOUND

Dynamoog
J. J. Perrey and G. Sigrist
Experimental electronic moods. (JH)

HISTORY: Founded in France in 1974 by Louis Delacour, former label manager of MP2000. Sub label of Neuilly and shares some releases with Mondiophone. OUTPUT: Approximately eighty releases, with a vast array of sounds and ideas. Some LPs rebadged from Neuilly and some sublicensing with Brull. STYLE: Mainly futuristic, progressive and electronic. MUSICIANS OF NOTE: Yan Tregger, Georges Rodi, Camille Sauvage. SLEEVES: From graphics to obscure photographic oddities and collages. Some LPs repackaged for Canada in printed 'disco bags'.

DANY

René Eiffel and his Orchestra
Various artists
Light, easy, orchestral. (JT)

Pop Electronique
Cecil Leuter
Creasound re-badging. (JG)

Informatic 2000
Roger Roger and Georges Teperino
Futuristic synth work c.1982. (FM)

HISTORY: Small early 1970s Italian pop label with a limited run of library LPs. See also Pinciana. OUTPUT: Somewhere in the order of ten LPs. STYLE: Jazz, easy, some light experimentation. MUSICIANS OF NOTE: Bonfanti, René Eiffel. SLEEVES: Graphic, basic, effective.

DENEB

Antico... Ma Non Tropo
Antonio Ricardo Luciano
Economic period sounds. (JT)

HISTORY: Started in 1970, part of the original Canopo label, merging into the larger Flipper group mid-1970s. Sublicensing to St Germain Des Prés. OUTPUT: Small catalogue (less than thirty LPs) of interesting library recordings. Sought after LPs. STYLE: Progressive, jazzy, experimental, easy. MUSICIANS OF NOTE: Alessandro Alessandroni, Antonio Ricardo Luciani. SLEEVES: Early sleeves have graphic lion motif, later LPs have simple colour and graphic sleeves.

DEVEGA

Effetti Sonori Musica Elettronica
Oskar Sala etc.
Important electronic recordings. (JT)

HISTORY: Italian label founded in Milan, c.1972. Possibly started by a German composer as many artists on the label are German. OUTPUT: Range of diverse music, catalogue numbering would suggest less than twenty LPs produced. Some very rare indeed. STYLE: Electronics, experimentals, easy listening, light orchestrals, jazz, funk. MUSICIANS OF NOTE: Joy Unlimited, Oskar Sala, Angel 'Pocho' Gatti. SLEEVES: Simple, sparse typography on plain or coloured backgrounds. Some graphics, such as film strips.

TV Suite
Peter Fenn and John Hawksworth
From cold stillness to disjointed fear. (I)

Colours
Peter Reno
A musical trip through the rainbow. (JT)

HISTORY: Hugely important independent label, founded in London in 1909. Library recordings originally recorded on 35mm open-track film, then later pressed on 78rpm; 10" 33rpm series began c.1960, then quickly moved into 12" 33rpm pressings. See also Hudson, Rouge, Sylvester, Timing and Musique Pour L'Image. OUTPUT: Over eight hundred releases across 10" and 12" LPs, including a small catalogue of SFX, plus earlier 78rpm pressings. Some sublicensing from Musique Pour L'Image for the Sylvester sub label, interesting set of collaborative licensing with Timing. STYLE: Themes and backgrounds covering every conceivable musical style. MUSICIANS OF NOTE: Alan Hawkshaw, Alan Parker, Nick Ingham, Jimmy Page, Basil Kirchin, Pete Reno, Johnny Hawksworth, Stanley Myers, Stéphane Grappelli, Reg Tilsley, Stanley Black, Roger Webb. SLEEVES: Early 10" recordings have generic 'paper bag' style design with type variations. More illustrative designs continued throughout the 1970s and early 1980s. Long series of distinctive red house sleeves, and red / white / blue 'fanfare' sleeves. Early cover art by Rolph Webster, later 1970s sleeves mostly by Nick Bantock. FAMOUS CUES: 'The Gallery' from *Vision On*, various *Sweeney* dramatics, *Monty Python*, *Roobarb & Custard*, *Emmanuelle*, all *Dawn Of The Dead* incidentals, *Man About The House*, *Van der Valk*, *Witchfinder General* score.

The Wild One
Basil Kirchin's London studio group, Jimmy Page features.
Early 'paper bag' style 10" sleeve. (JT)

Busy Quayside
Jack Trombey
Unusual, lively industrials. 10". (JT)

Journey Into Sound
Keith Papworth
Light compositions with acoustic effects. 10". (JT)

High Speed Jazz
Renaud and Gainsbourg International Jazz Group.
Lively jazz. 10". (JT)

Band 8
Herbert Chappell
Small band novelties. (JT)

Metal Sunrise
P. Avray
Continental small group sounds. (FM)

A Rose For Dracula
C. Staker
Dark horror and drama. (JM)

Bite Hard
Johnny Hawksworth
Powerful modern sounds. (JM)

Dinky Doo
Keith Papworth and the London Studio Group
Early and happy novelties. (LV)

Highlight
Hugo De Groot
Small group impressions. 10" release. (JT)

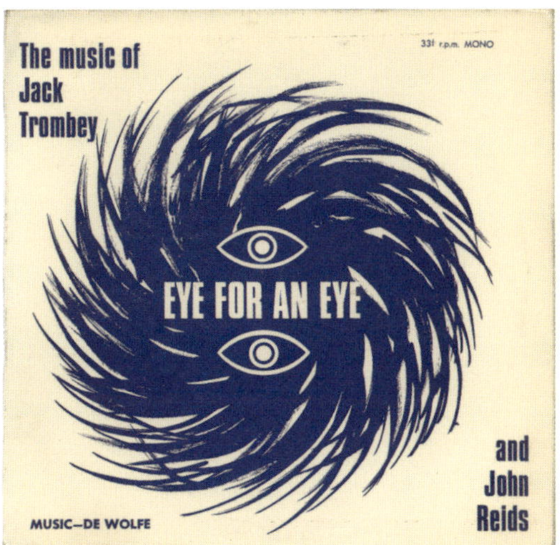

Assignment London
Jack Trombey and John Reids
Sounds for swinging espionage. (JT)

Eye For An Eye
Jack Trombey and John Reids
Includes 'Girl In The Dark', the theme from *Callan*. (JT)

Don't Lose Your Cool
Kirchin, Nathan, Coleman
Otherwordly jazz and unexpected vocals. (JT)

Johnny Hawksworth's Caribbean Sound
The Coconutters
Lively exotics. (JT)

Natural Break
Bright Spark
Funky, carefree, disco. (JT)

New Generation
Laurence Stephen Orchestra
Modern sounds. (S)

Who's Gonna Buy? The Lemon Dips
Johnny Hawksworth and Pete Reno
Classic 1960s beat and psych. (C)

Z Patrol
Reg Tilsley
Tough crime jazz. (C)

Forest Of Evil
The Slipstream Group
Early synthesiser and drum machine cues, foreboding themes. (C)

Even More Electric Banana
Includes members of The Pretty Things
Third LP in the Banana Series.
1960s beat and hard psych with vocals. (C)

Rubber Riff
Line-up features part of the band Soft Machine
Modern rock. (JM)

Dangerous Connection
Drama, action, suspense.
Small group sounds. (JM)

Feeling High
The Barry Stoller Band
Funky group sounds. (JM)

Weekend World
Simon Park
Dramatic themes. (JD)

8 Days A Week
The Unit Seven Band
Easy going backgrounds. (JM)

Synthesiser Contact
Pete Reno
Modern small group sounds. (JM)

Black Pearl
Alan Hawkshaw and Alan Parker
Soulful, pacey and fresh sounds. (MG)

Quietly with Johann
Reg Tilsley
Classics and novelty pop. 10" release. (JT)

Push Button
Contemporary electronic cues.
Sleeve by Kate Kelly. (MG)

Output
Small orchestral, industrial sounds. (JM)

Vocal Shades And Tones
Barbara Moore
Classic scat LP. (JT)

Space Drive
C. Evans-Ironside
Futuristic concepts. (MG)

HOGAN,
THE
HAWK
&
DIRTY
JOHN
CROWN
STRIPTEASE
BOOKS
48
BOOK SHOP
music de wolfe

Hogan, The Hawk & Dirty John Crown
Alan Parker and W. Parrish
Up to date group sounds. (JM)

Sun High
Simon Park
Modern synthesiser dramatics. (JM)

Mind On The Run
Basil Kirchin and John Coleman
Paranoid links and bridges. 10" release. (JT)

New Decade
The London Studio Group
Fine dramatics. (JM)

Go Go Volume 1
J. C. Pierric and M. Chadcar
Oddball synth jams. (JD)

HISTORY: Italian, late 1970s. OUTPUT: Only five LPs traced. STYLE: Electronic, disco, French reggae. MUSICIANS OF NOTE: J. C. Pierric. SLEEVES: All sleeves feature dove and face image, with changes in colour and type.

DISC L'AGAMI

Les Splendid
Leo Petit / Michael Hington
Groovy sounds. (JT)

HISTORY: Micro library label from Paris, c.1970. OUTPUT: One LP traced, very rare. STYLE: Progressive, modern pop, jazz. MUSICIANS OF NOTE: J. C. Pierric under pseudonym of M. Hington. SLEEVES: Two colours, simple typography.

DISC. WALDBERG

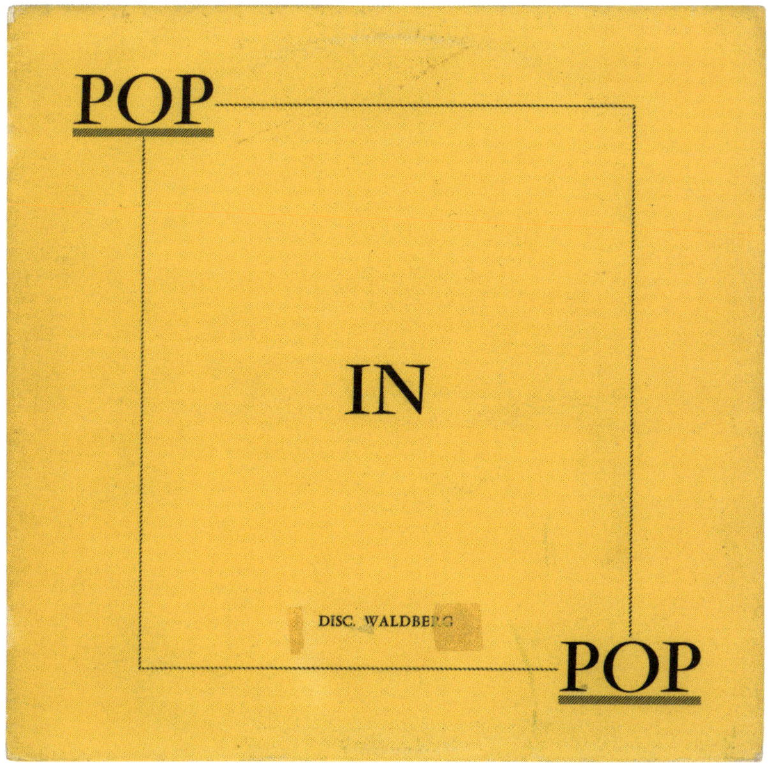

Pop In Pop
Claude Dauray
Subversive pop oddness. (JT)

HISTORY: Peculiar label from France, c.1970. OUTPUT: One LP traced, some distribution via Brull. STYLE: Uneasy listening, some dynamic pop sounds. MUSICIANS OF NOTE: Claude Dauray. SLEEVES: Simple but elegant two colour design.

DISQUES BAGATELLE

DRIVE IN

Musical Environments
The Mercators
Lively fusions. Eurobeat sticker. (JT)

Folk Celebrations
Jean-Pierre Sabar
Exotic things. Eurobeat sticker. (JT)

Chess Pops
Fritz Münzer's Sound Factory
Back cover is a chess board. Game on. (JT)

HISTORY: Mysterious French label, started c.1968. OUTPUT: Just two LPs sent out for synchronisation via international sub-publishers. STYLE: Jazzy, folk, world. MUSICIANS OF NOTE: The Mercators, Jean-Pierre Sabar. SLEEVES: Both sleeves with the same artwork in different colours, often found with sublicensing stickers.

HISTORY: Rare German label from the mid-1970s. OUTPUT: Very small, catalogue numbers suggest up to seventeen LPs produced, but few have been traced. STYLE: Jazz, easy. MUSICIANS OF NOTE: Perry London. SLEEVES: Plain typography, with some graphics and illustration. Quite conceptual.

Franco Chiari Volume II
Franco Chiari
A second helping of groovy sounds. (JT)

Doggy Bag
Walter Rizzati
Some harmless sounds. Eurobeat sticker. (JT)

HISTORY: Part of the Beat record company, based in Rome. See also New Bingo, Pentaphon, Pony and Gemini. OUTPUT: Mainly soundtrack issues, but the occasional foray into library LPs. Over twenty LPs traced. STYLE: Light classical, jazz, easy listening. MUSICIANS OF NOTE: Franco Chiari. SLEEVES: No house style. But geometric painting artwork by Cavallaro also used by Beat for at least one release.

EBONITE

Album 18
Persuasive Jazz
Includes covers of Stevie Wonder. (JT)

HISTORY: Unusual American label, a small part of the large UK based President record label. OUTPUT: Over one hundred and fifty LPs pressed in the Ebonite 'library' series, but it remains unclear if these were simply for home use, syncronisation or a bizarre tax avoidance scheme. STYLE: Some unique recordings, many extended cover versions of jazz, soul, funk and disco classics, all pressed across several different series – *Intimate Disco*, *Persuasive Jazz*, etc. MUSICIANS OF NOTE: Most LPs have no artist names mentioned. SLEEVES: Each series has the standard two disc op art image, colours change for each series.

E.C.A.P

Top Instrumental Music 6
Tany Turens
Light, easy, orchestral. (JS)

HISTORY: Early 1970s French label, based in Paris. OUTPUT: Small disco / pop output, later moving into library music. A series of eight instrumental library albums pressed. These remain quite obscure. STYLE: Interesting and diverse instrumentals. MUSICIANS OF NOTE: Tany Turens, The Chris Oward Group, some amateurs. SLEEVES: Set of spiralling squares on all LPs, with changes in tone and colour. FAMOUS CUES: The *Stop, Look, Listen* music.

Mostra Collettiva
Various artists
Various styles from jazz to drama. 1972. (JT)

Antico Mondo Greco Romano
Gisteri / Santany
Fine ancient and minimal sounds. (JT)

HISTORY: Rome based label from 1971. OUTPUT: Just five LPs traced across the 1970s, but catalogue numbers suggest perhaps fifteen LPs made. Rare. STYLE: Bizarre range of styles from easy to historical ideas. MUSICIANS OF NOTE: Gisteri (Rino De Fillipi), Romolo Grano. SLEEVES: Early sleeves green or black with simple stave design. Later issues use simple graphics and paintings. Unusually heavy card.

EDI-PAN

Jumping
Fogù, Taormina
Funny jazz. (JT)

Tempo sospeso
Bruno Nicolai
Fuzz guitar led thriller and giallo horror themes. (C)

HISTORY: 1970s label started in Rome by Bruno Nicolai, issuing mainly film music, with library offshoot. Parent label of Gemelli. OUTPUT: Over thirty albums found on the MPS library catalogue. STYLE: Odd, experimental, dark and brooding themes, travel and conflict a speciality. MUSICIANS OF NOTE: Leo Flag (Bruno Nicolai), Fred Bongusto. SLEEVES: Mostly photographic, some montages.

EDIPHON

Brani Vari
Luigi Zito
Lively jazz and improvisations. (JP)

Musica Del Nostro Tempo
Various Artists
Bucolic sounds. (S)

HISTORY: Super obscure Italian label, active c.1970. OUTPUT: Only two LPs traced to date. Very rare. STYLE: Experimental, avant-garde. MUSICIANS OF NOTE: Luigi Zito, Vittorio Nadalin. SLEEVES: Simply typography.

EDIZIONI CICLAMINO

Atmosfere
Melchiori / Luciani
Average instrumental atmospherics. (JP)

Fly In 5 Dimensione / Planet Beta
Melchiori
Two track cosmic concept. (JP)

HISTORY: Italian label based in Florence, started in 1979 and rising from the ashes of Altomusic. See also Floppi Rekord. OUTPUT: At least four LPs. STYLE: Light electronics, ambient sounds. Interesting for the period. MUSICIANS OF NOTE: Marco Melchiori (Teisco), A. Riccardo Luciani. SLEEVES: Three use the flower image in various colours. The other sleeve has a 'space' image.

EDIZIONI MUSICALI ELETTRA

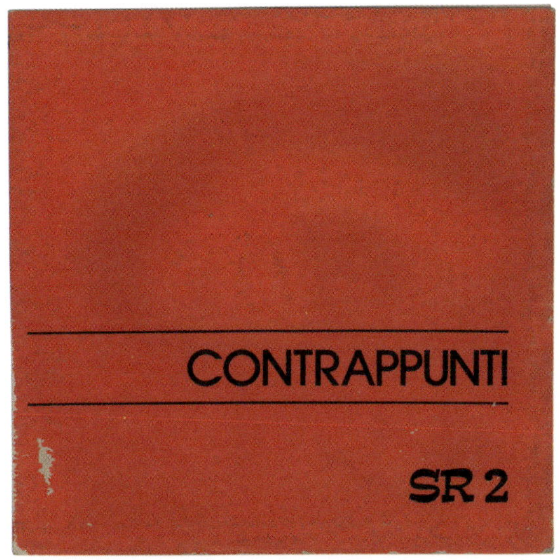

Contrappunti
Niliomi
Experimental sounds and compositions. (S)

Flash Back
Donaway
Classical, experimental. (S)

HISTORY: Library project by experimental Italian record label. OUTPUT: We have traced four LPs to date. Very few others likely to exist. Rare. Interesting to note that the company produced two separate catalogues of library LPs, the red series (SR for Serierossa) and the green series (SV for Serieverde). STYLE: Electronic, experimental, concrete, classical. MUSICIANS OF NOTE: Donaway, Niliomi. SLEEVES: Simple title, catalogue number and line. All sleeves are gatefold with spaces for production notes to be written.

ELEKTRA LIBRARY

Dramatic Cue & Mood Music Volume 1
Robert Kreis
Classical drama cues. (JT)

HISTORY: Seemingly unsuccessful venture into library music production by American recording giant. OUTPUT: Just two LPs found, from 1964. STYLE: Both standard and intriguing mood music cues, beds and stings. MUSICIANS OF NOTE: Both LPs by Robert Kreis and his orchestra. SLEEVES: Impressive design for the period, by William S. Harvey.

EMBER

2000 Weeks
Don Burrows
Jazz moods.
Rare Australian soundtrack issued as library. 1969. (SS)

HISTORY: Part of the large Ember music label, London, mid-1960s. OUTPUT: At least forty LPs, many international albums repressed as library, including wholesale LPs from Italy and Australia. A series of at least ten LPs all sublicensed from Vedette, with original pressings simply slipped into Ember sleeves. STYLE: Some impressive jazz and film music. MUSICIANS OF NOTE: Tubby Hayes, Armando Sciascia, Tommy Whittle. SLEEVES: Blue with white type, area for catalogue number to be handwritten. LP titles and tracklistings pasted on the back. Some also appear in standard Vedette tricolour sleeves.

EPERVIER

Travelling Flash
André Lutereau
Various strings, skits and percussion. (JD)

HISTORY: Paris pop label started c.1970, with small library music output. OUTPUT: Approximately ten LPs produced. STYLE: Mainly small group sessions, everything from jazz to circus themes, with travel a speciality. MUSICIANS OF NOTE: André Lutereau, Michel Lorin. SLEEVES: Early sleeves with photographic distortions, later sleeves using colour graphics and photography. No distinctive house style. Early releases used photographs of artists on reverse.

FAMA

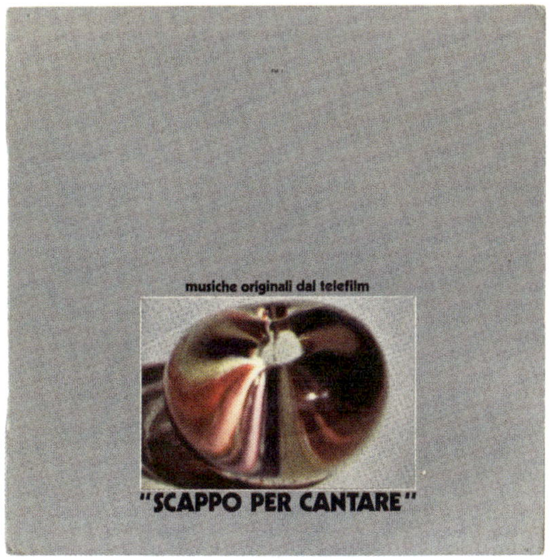

Suoni Di Una Città' Nuovaserie No. 1
Teresa Luciani
Ambient and textured found sound. (C)

Scappo Per Cantare
Giuliano Sorgini
Fascinating wordless vocal moods. (S)

HISTORY: Obscure offshoot of RCA Italy, with some specific releases for library use. OUTPUT: According to catalogue numbers, at least twelve on the FM library series were issued. Rare. STYLE: Experimental, jazz, electronics, concrete. MUSICIANS OF NOTE: Rino De Filippi, Maria Teresa Luciani, Carlo Pes. SLEEVES: Photographic distortions, both simple and bizarre graphics. No house style.

FIRMAMENTO

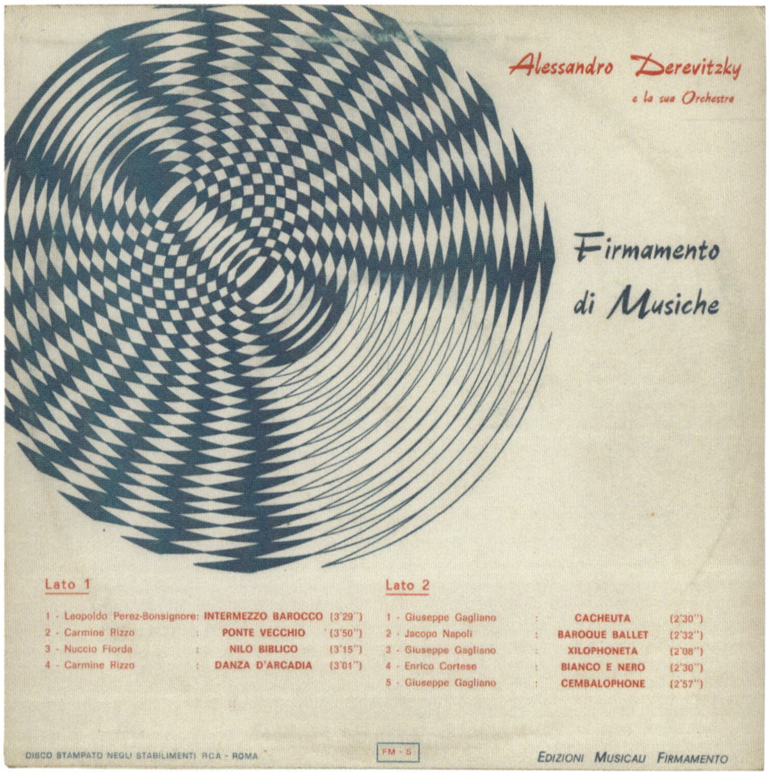

Firmamento Di Musiche
Alessandro Derevitsky And His Orchestra
Fine compositions by Umiliani, Tamponi etc played by orchestra. (JS)

HISTORY: Tiny label from Italy, late 1960s. Possible connection to RTV. OUTPUT: Catalogue numbers suggest up to ten LPs produced. STYLE: Experimental, pastoral. MUSICIANS OF NOTE: Bruno Battisti D'Amario. SLEEVES: Op Art circles and typography.

FLAM

Patchwork
The Phantoms
Groovy groups. (JT)

Softly Softly
Fabor and Savina
Light and beautiful atmospheres. (JT)

HISTORY: 1980s Italian label, offshoot of Fonovideo. See also Ring, Hard and World. OUTPUT: Intriguing and diverse catalogue, over twenty LPs issued from 1981 onwards. STYLE: Standard dramatics to cues for comedy and electronics. MUSICIANS OF NOTE: Oscar Rocchi, Carlo Savina, Fabio Fabor. SLEEVES: No house style, an unpredictable mix of photography, graphics, art and fonts.

Underground Mood 9
Roberto Conrado, E. De Angelis
Amazing rare jazz and ideas. (JS)

HISTORY: Lively Italian label, started c.1971. Part of the Canopo group, merging into the Flipper oganisation by the mid-1970s. OUTPUT: Catalogue numbering suggests at least twenty LPs produced, but these are very scarce. Possibly some sublicensing, see Vi Di Elle. STYLE: Easy listening, hip psychedelia, dramatics, some fine industrials. MUSICIANS OF NOTE: Alessandro Alessandroni, Raskovich (Sorgini), The Cast Five, Daniela Casa. SLEEVES: Early issues have butterfly sleeves, later editions have simple, bold typography.

Dragon
Rimauri
Futuristic electronic ideas. (JP)

D.O.C.
Rimauri
More futuristic electronic ideas. (JP)

HISTORY: Italian label, from the late 1980s. See also Edizioni Ciclamino, and Altomusic. OUTPUT: Just these two LPs. STYLE: Experimental, cosmic, odd. MUSICIANS OF NOTE: Rimauri (AKA Marco Melchiori / AKA Teisco). SLEEVES: Dynamic graphic statements printed in two colours.

FLOWER

Drammatico Per Quartetto D'Archi
Paolo Renosto
Simple drama cues. (JT)

HISTORY: Small and interesting Italian library label, set up in 1972, part of the Canopo group, merging into the Flipper organisation by the mid-1970s. OUTPUT: Catalogue numbers suggest at least sixty LPs released, about half have been traced and documented. Some cross pollination and distribution via MP2000. STYLE: Jazz, world, folk, experimental. MUSICIANS OF NOTE: Paolo Renosto, Tamponi, Alessandroni, Eric Framond, Oscar Rocchi, Rino De Filippi. SLEEVES: Early sleeves have coloured circle design, some with illustration. Later editions use generic pink typography, identical in style to later Octopus, Canopo and Flirt graphics.

FLY

La Pace
Giacomo Dell'Orso
Rare wordless vocal and jazz cues. (S)

HISTORY: Italian, founded in the late 1960s by producer, director and philanthropist Aldo Sinezio. OUTPUT: Small but important. A handful of LPs, all very rare and desirable. STYLE: Primarily jazz based library music. MUSICIANS OF NOTE: Gianni Mazza, Oscar Lindok, Santucci Scoppa. SLEEVES: Early sleeves have the flash / blurred flower image with interesting typography. Later pressing are illustration and graphic based.

FONIT / FONIT CETRA

7000 Hi International Fi Series
Quarta Pagina
Braen / Raskovich
Fine psychedelic drama. (S)

7001 Hi International Fi Series
Atmosfere
Rino De Filippi etc
Peculiar and dark vibes. (JT)

7002 Hi International Fi Series
Various artists
World music and folkloric. (JT)

HISTORY: Important Italian label started in 1959 with amalgamation of Fonit and Cetra music houses. See also Usignolo and Goldfinger. OUTPUT: Main library based LPs are issued under the large Usignolo (Nightingale) Series. But under the Fonit banner there seem to be occasional forays into library, such as the *Commenti Musicali* Series, also the important *Hi International Fi Series* of at least thirteen LPs from the early 1970s that all begin at the number 7000. There are also some confusing crossovers and idiosyncrasies with the Usignolo and Goldfinger catalogues. STYLE: Standard library music ideas, some amazing jazz and progressive recordings under the *Hi International Fi Series*. MUSICIANS OF NOTE: Stefano Torossi, Giuliano Sorgini, Alessandro Alessandroni. SLEEVES: Some splash / spin painting. Some two colour period graphics and illustration for the 1980s *Commenti Musicali* LPs. All Special 3000 Series LPs have individual artwork.

7004 Hi International Fi Series
Various artists
Solo instruments and vocals. (S)

Arte Moderna Commenti Musicali Series
Rava, Tommasi, Ortolani
Modern jazz, modern classical. (JT)

TV Musica
Trecca
TV and film music for synchronisation. (JT)

Max Raffeng No.6
Fabio Fabor under pseudonym
Light jazz. (JT)

PoP-PaRaPhReNiA.....
Rocchi and Godi
Fine psych and pop.
MP2000 sublicense sticker. (JG)

Woman's Colours
The Barigozzi Group
Pop jazz themes. (JG)

HISTORY: One of the small Italian sub labels of Edizioni Musicali Minstrel, in Rome. Linked also to Flam, Hard, Ring and World. OUTPUT: From catalogue numbers, twenty-seven LPs have been issued. Some distribution via MP2000. STYLE: Mood music from easy to pop, specialising in jazz. MUSICIANS OF NOTE: Max Raffeng, Giancarlo Barigozzi. SLEEVES: Intruiging typography, sometimes with stock photos and colour tints. No definitive house style.

Stressorama
Fabio Fabor / Giancarlo Barigozzi / Oscar Rocchi
Anxious jazz. (S)

Sport Music
Garnegy and Maties
Electronic sport adventures. (JT)

HISTORY: Small French pop label offshoot of Carrere Records. OUTPUT: Just one LP made for synchronisation. STYLE: Electronic sport music. MUSICIANS OF NOTE: Garnegy and Maties. SLEEVES: Classic 1980s sport graphics.

FOREVER RECORDS

Astromusic
Marcello Giombini
Commercial cosmic space compositions as library. (JT)

HISTORY: Small Italian label set up c.1980. OUTPUT: Rock, pop and electronic releases, with a short series of FVLPs made for library use. STYLE: Plugged-in global themes. MUSICIANS OF NOTE: Marcello Giombini. SLEEVES: Some simple graphics, others more complicated with full colour artwork and die cut features.

FRANCIS DAY & HUNTER

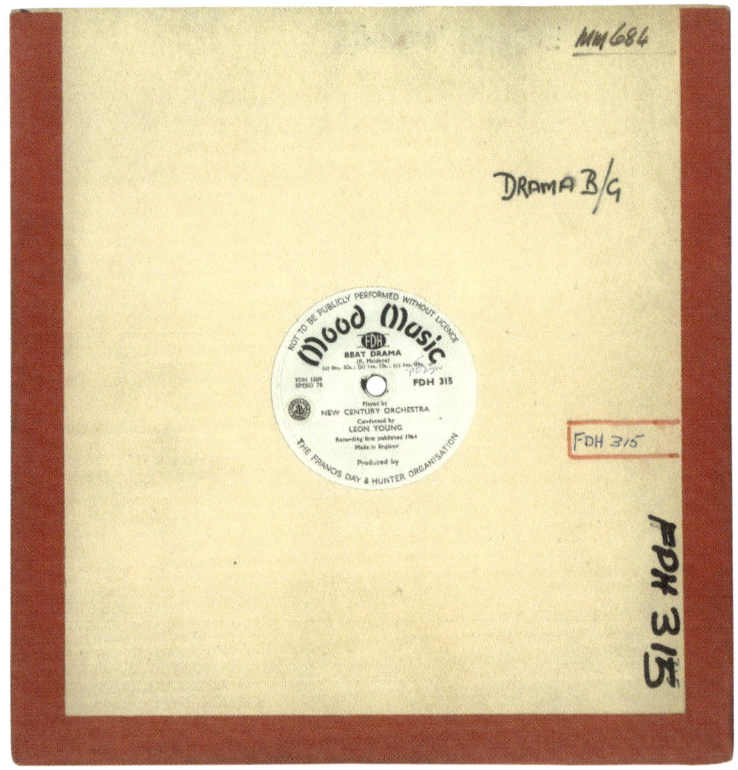

Beat Drama
R. Maidana
Dramatic industrials. (JP)

HISTORY: Large publishing house moving into library music production, from the mid-1960s onwards. OUTPUT: Average sized catalogue issued on both 10"and 12" LP. Over thirty LPs, but surprisingly rare. STYLE: Jazz, pop classical, some dramatics, easy. MUSICIANS OF NOTE: Sam Fonteyn, Derek Mason. SLEEVES: Blue sleeve with simple black and white typography.

FREESOUND

Motivations
Sam Fonteyn
Easy and jazz industrials. (SG)

Philopsis
Jacky Giordano
Mechanical marches and drums, 1975. (JT)

HISTORY: Classic French label, founded in Paris in 1973. Part of the Ambient Musicale Illustration Sonore and in the UK associated with Harmonic and Studio G. OUTPUT: Just six LPs produced. STYLE: Free, jazz based, artistic and dramatic. MUSICIANS OF NOTE: Jacky Giordano, Yan Tregger. SLEEVES: Interesting collage with good typography.

Challenger
Jacky Giordano
Percussion, electronics. 1974. (S)

Understood
Jacky Giordano and Robert Hermel
Includes *The faded charm of father sax*. 1973. (S)

Schifters
Jacky Giordano and Yan Tregger
Wah-wah and more. 1974. (S)

Ovation
Various artists
Jazz, rock, electronics and more. 1973. (S)

Interiezioni
Luigia Sordini
Modern classical, jazz, progressive. (JD)

Varie Atmosfere Da Interni
Giuliano Sorgini
Unusual jazzy vibes. (S)

HISTORY: Small Italian library label from the 1970s. OUTPUT: Only three LPs traced, catalogue numbers suggest at least eight were planned. STYLE: Experimental dramatics. MUSICIANS OF NOTE: Giuliano Sorgini, Luciano Simoncini. SLEEVES: Simple graphics and typography.

Espressioni
Bruno Nicolai
Moody dramatics. (JT)

Spector
Victor
Electronic compositions. (JT)

HISTORY: Set up by Bruno Nicolai in 1970 as part of the larger Edi-Pan label. OUTPUT: Over thirty LPs produced, mainly original film music and experimental issues, but large numbers of albums sent across Europe re-badged for library usage. STYLE: Mainly dark and experimental, some electronics. MUSICIANS OF NOTE: Bruno Nicolai, Ennio Morricone, Egisto Macchi. SLEEVES: Thick card sleeves with rich and varied graphics, photography and typography. Regular variations of logo. Some usage of modern art, including Kandinsky and Mondrian.

Rendez Vous
Bruno Nicolai
Dark, brooding, urban jazz themes. (JT)

Voix
Egisto Macchi
Eerie treated choral vocals. (C)

Thomas
Amedeo Tommasi
Super jazz, vocals. (JT)

I Gres Volume 2
Lo Turco and Rizzati
Various jazz themes. (JT)

Insight Modulation
Zanagoria
Dark jazz. (I)

Contro Fase
Ennio Morricone
Experimental, treated piano, electronics. (JT)

GEMINI MUSIC LIBRARY

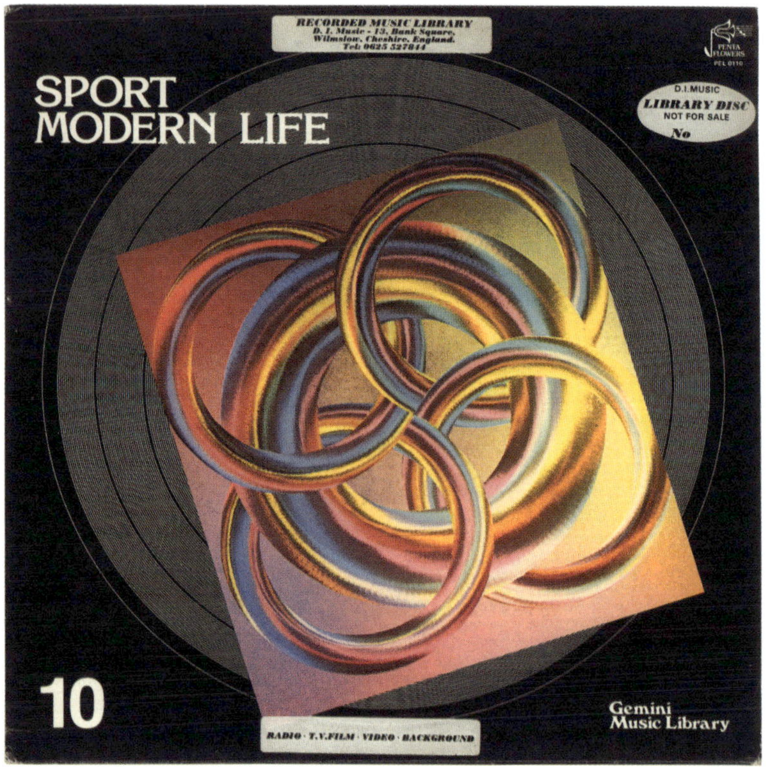

Sport Modern Life
Elvio Monti
Winning mid-1980s compositions. (JT)

HISTORY: Mid-1980s Italian library label, also known as Penta Flowers, an offshoot of Beat. See also Duse, Pentaphon. Pony and New Bingo. OUTPUT: Medium sized vinyl output. At least twenty releases. STYLE: Classic library themes and ideas. MUSICIANS OF NOTE: Alessandro Alessandroni, Space Sensation Group. SLEEVES: Black sleeves with grey 'film can' and graphic or photographic devices.

GEVOX

A La Carte
Lauth Quartet
Beat, jazz, Latin.
Rare white label. (S)

HISTORY: Italian label from Genoa, mid-1970s. OUTPUT: Small number of library releases amidst a catalogue of pop, classical and jazz. Rare to find. Possibly some 7" records released for syncronisation too. Both Italian and German musicians involved. STYLE: Jazz, pastoral, experimental, some international sounds. MUSICIANS OF NOTE: Hans Zauberfinger, Lauth Quartet. SLEEVES: Unusual geometric stylings on disco bags, normally one or two colours. Some flat coloured sleeves with plain typography.

GLOBE

10 Situazioni
Dino Piana and Oscar Valdambrini
Lively jazz. (S)

Sensazioni No.1
Chimenti, Ciangherotti
Psychedelia for the TV. (JP)

HISTORY: Rome based label from 1971. OUTPUT: Small and diverse output. Catalogue numbers would suggest five LPs were produced. Poor distribution. Rare records. STYLE: Psychedelics, jazz, experimental recordings. MUSICIANS OF NOTE: Oscar Valdambrini. SLEEVES: A bizarre mix – strange graphic illustrations and typography.

Turn On
Frank Mantis Group
Fine contemporary sounds. (JG)

Orion 2000
Pete Thomas
Classic 1975 recording. (JD)

HISTORY: Mid-1970s German based label, started by Ralph Marco. Possibly licensed internationally by Telemusic. OUTPUT: Approximately one hundred LPs produced. STYLE: Mixture of obvious and classic library styles, from ragtime to love thematics. MUSICIANS OF NOTE: Klaus Weiss, Pete Thomas, Ralph Marco, Siegfried Schwab, David Snell, Gershon Kingsley. SLEEVES: Basic graphics, typography, some were pressed with disco sleeves, and a whole series with 'film camera' artwork. Some LPs come with unusual printed inner sleeve. FAMOUS CUES: BBC Radio 3 cricket interval music.

Make Friends
Ralph Marco Band
Unusual twisted beat themes. (JG)

Sound Music Album No.11
Klaus Weiss
Progressive drum action. (JT)

UST 270 **Nei Confini Dello Scibile**
Giuliano Sorgini
Ambient moody electronics. (JT)

UST 335
Giuliano Sorgini
Fine dramatics. Some percussion. (GJ)

HISTORY: Obscure little publishing offshoot of the Fonit Cetra / Usignolo catalogues. OUTPUT: At least seven LPs traced. STYLE: Experimental, dramatic, jazzy. MUSICIANS OF NOTE: Giuliano Sorgini, Alberto Baldan Bembo. SLEEVES: Most follow the form of the Usignolo sleeves, and often multiple company logos appear.

Reportages Musicali No.1
De Luca, Cortese
Rare giallo sounds. (JP)

Ritmo Dell' Industria No.2
Alessandro Alessandroni
More modern manufacturing compositions. (JS)

Ritmo Dell' Industria No.1
Franco Tamponi / Michael Giacchino
Modern manufacturing compositions. (JS)

HISTORY: Late 1960s label from Italy, part of the Leonardi group. OUTPUT: Small but very desirable. Less than twenty LPs exist. Very hard to find. STYLE: Jazz, progressive, unusual. MUSICIANS OF NOTE: Giuliano Sorgini, Giancarlo Bizzi, Alessandro Alessandroni. SLEEVES: Unusual graphics, some hand drawn typography.

GRIFO

Signori: L'Orchestra!
Includes Sorgini, Fusco and Funaro
Simple classical cues. (JT)

Vetrina Musciale
Franco Potenza
Exotic marvels. (JT)

HISTORY: Short lived independent Italian label, started in 1968. OUTPUT: Currently only ten albums traced but catalogue may run to twenty. At least five in the *Vetrina Musicale* (Musical Showcase) series. STYLE: Jazzy, experimental, classical, choral, exotic, bananas. MUSICIANS OF NOTE: Ugo Fusco, Franco Potenza. SLEEVES: Some illustration, but mainly simple, effective and occasionally dynamic graphic styles.

Mister Marco's Music
Ralph Marco Band
Various contemporary mood cues. (GJ)

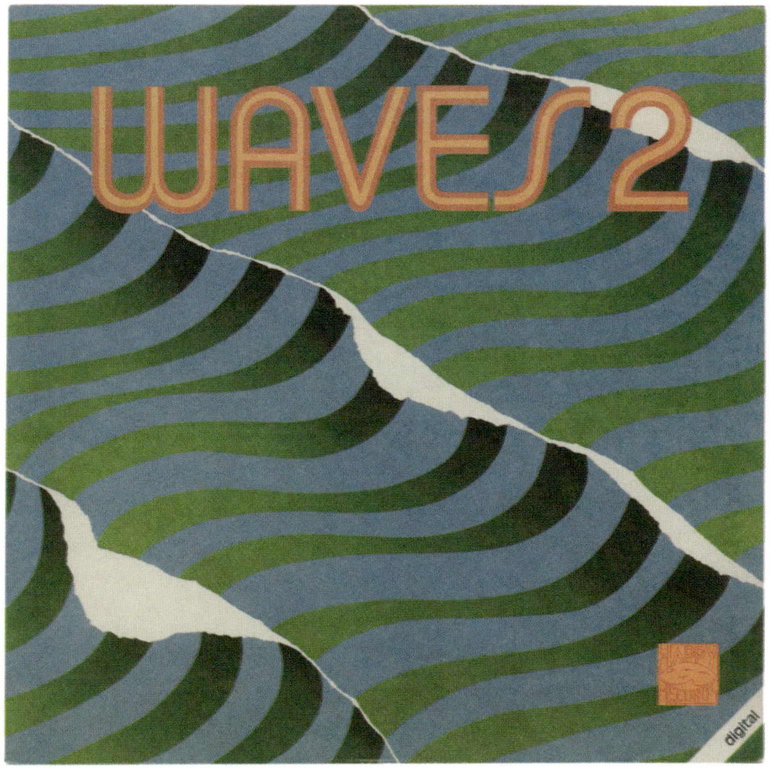

Waves 2
Ralph Marco and Friends
Casual sounds. (JT)

HISTORY: **German library label started in 1974. Part of the Golden Ring library empire.** OUTPUT: **Small number of releases.** STYLE: **Jazz, jazz funk, cosmic.** MUSICIANS OF NOTE: **Ralph Marco, Frank Mantis, Werner Drexler.** SLEEVES: **Graphic effects, normally two colour designs.**

HARD

Aquarium
Fabio Fabor
Modern jazz aquatics. (JT)

HISTORY: Small Italian subsidiary label of Minstrel Music, started in 1980. Linked also to Bam, Flam, Fonovideo, Ring and World. OUTPUT: Less than ten LPs. STYLE: Modern classical and jazz. MUSICIANS OF NOTE: Fabio Fabor and his pseudonyms. SLEEVES: Stock photography with type.

HARMONIC

Music For Effect
H. Possega
10" release. (JT)

Studies in Drama
Martin Bottcher and Pete Thomas
Harmonic paint splatter sleeve. (JT)

HISTORY: Established in the mid-1960s as part of the large and diverse Brull publishing house and distribution network. OUTPUT: Many quite confusing releases across both 10" and 12" LPs. Lots of international sub licensing and cross-pollination. Catalogue numbers begin with a variety of CB prefixes. STYLE: Easy, jazz, world music, light orchestral, experimental. MUSICIANS OF NOTE: Roland Kovac, Ronnie Ross, Gert Wilden. SLEEVES: 10" LPs mostly have the standard film strip sleeves. LPs use spin painting design in varying colours or standard single colour sleeves (orange, purple, gold) with typography.

HIBOU

Hibou Volume 1
Philippe Bréjean
Suspense and mystery themes. (JH)

HISTORY: Productions et éditions Hibou, Paris, late 1960s onwards. Hibou translates as 'Owl'. See also Sysmo. OUTPUT: Thirteen LPs traced. Quite scarce. STYLE: Broad range of musical ideas and concepts, from fantasy to drama and music for children. MUSICIANS OF NOTE: Philippe Bréjean, Yvon Rioland. SLEEVES: Owl artwork with simple colour and type variations. Artwork by Hélène Courtaigne.

HOMÈRE

Homère Instrumental
Jean-Michel Lorgere
Modern compositions. (JG)

HISTORY: Known as Homère Instrumental, this small Paris label was started in the late 1960s. OUTPUT: Ten library LPs traced. Poor distribution, so LPs are rare. STYLE: Jazz, bossa nova, light classical, experimental. MUSICIANS OF NOTE: Yan Tregger, Dany Doriz. SLEEVES: Simple typography, a small series with the 'Homère Man' graphic, some collage.

Karaté K. No.1
Pierre Louvet
Progressive jazz sounds. (JG)

Magnum
Jan Tregger
Pop diversion.
Artwork by Jan Tregger. (JH)

HUDSON MUSIC

Headline
Barbara Moore
Modern orchestral pieces. (JD)

Mindbender
Avant-jazz.
Artwork by Ken Hutchinson Associates. (JM)

Dramaturgy / Cosmogony
Paul Lemel
Dramatic atmospheres for the walking dead. (JT)

HISTORY: Company started in London, mid-1930s, producing strict tempo dance music. Acquired by De Wolfe Music which produced library LPs from around 1965 onwards. See also De Wolfe. OUTPUT: According to catalogue numbers, forty-nine LPs have been produced, along with a short series of 7″ EPs . STYLE: Fine mood music, electronics, jazz, experimentals. MUSICIANS OF NOTE: Pete Reno, Pierre Arvay, Reg Tilsley, Peter Fenn. SLEEVES: As with later De Wolfe catalogue, graphics, freestyle illustration and photography. FAMOUS CUES: *Dawn Of The Dead* incidentals.

Disco Elettronico
Torallo
Intense plugged-in noise. (JP)

Climax Issue 1
Marega
Way out electronics. (JT)

MA-GI
Maurizio Bigio
Rhythms, harmonicas, drama. (S)

Suddenly
Ugo Busoni
Funky light orchestral sounds. (JT)

HISTORY: Small Italian imprint, part of the sprawling RCA library catalogue. OUTPUT: Only thirteen LPs traced to date. STYLE: Various, from electronics to global influenced concepts. MUSICIANS OF NOTE: Giovanni Tommaso, Ugo Busoni. SLEEVES: No house style, stock photography and type.

L'ILLUSTRATION MUSICALE

(IM)

IM 14 Various Traditional Backgrounds
Eddie Warner, Nino Nardini, Cecil Leuter
Diverse mood music. IM disco bag. (JT)

HISTORY: This Paris based 'Label of Modern Rhythms' was set up in the late 1960s by jazz pianist Eddie Warner. See also Musax. OUTPUT: A total of twenty-seven LPs were issued, and a white label of an unissued twenty-eighth has been located. STYLE: Jazz, experimental, quirky, electronic. MUSICIANS OF NOTE: Eddie Warner, Jacky Giordano, Johnny Hawksworth, Roger Roger. SLEEVES: Generic 'im' sleeves, some house bags. Different colourways. Simple logos with various graphic treatments. Sparse sleevenotes.

IM 25 **Sound Industrial**
Roger Roger (JD)

IM 26 **Organ Plus**
Jacky Giordano
Generic sleeve. (S)

IM 22 **Cops, Crooks and Spies**
Eddie Warner
Classic experimentals. (JD)

IML
(INTERNATIONAL MUSIC LABEL)

IML 02 **Drumo Vocalo**
Daniel Humair
Drums, vocals, special effects. (JH)

IML 04 **Hypnose**
Teddy Lasry
Dark, hypnotic sounds. (JD)

HISTORY: Paris based from early 1970s. Subsidiary of the Montparnasse label. OUTPUT: Only seven LPs traced to date. STYLE: Experimental, avant-garde, uneasy listening, progressive. MUSICIANS OF NOTE: Teddy Lasry, Daniel Humair, Bernard Lubat. SLEEVES: IML logo always used as shown. A mix of graphics and photography.

IMPALA

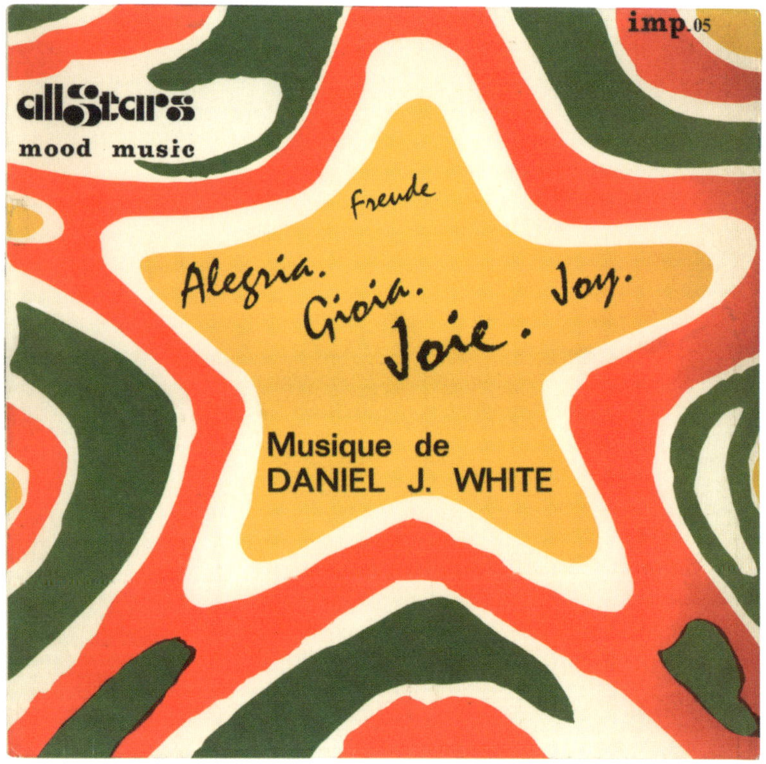

All Stars Mood Music Selection IMP05
Daniel J. White
Simple mood and pop sounds.
Includes *Naked Dames In Fur*. (JT)

HISTORY: Small Paris pop label dating from 1972, with tiny library output. OUTPUT: Based on catalogue numbers only five library LPs were made. Limited European distribution. STYLE: Pop and easy moods. MUSICIANS OF NOTE: Daniel J. White. SLEEVES: Star design in different colourways as well as simple block colours with typography.

IMPRESS

Gut Reaction!
Duncan Lamont
Fast, repetitive rhythms and moods. (S)

HISTORY: Originally formed in the 1950s by entrepreneur Gordon Barnes. Company name is an acronym of Inter-art Music Publishers. Acquired by Joseph Weinberger in the early 1970s when the company went bust. OUTPUT: Released a series of 10″ 78rpm recordings in the late 1950s, moved onto 33rpm in the 1960s, and finally onto 12″ vinyl in 1970. Catalogue numbers suggest in excess of one hundred releases STYLE: A broad range from light orchestral to easy listening and progressive, dramatic sounds. MUSICIANS OF NOTE: Freddie Phillips, Syd Dale, Don Harper, Duncan Lamont. SLEEVES: LPs sleeves in generic blue and white house bag, with simple changes in artists and title.

INDISPENSABLE MUSIC LIBRARY

Volume 18 No.2
Bruce Clarke
Bright and easy cues. (JT)

HISTORY: Australian jazz master Bruce Clarke's own music library company. This library label, one of at least two he created, was started c.1970, in Melbourne, and sprang from his Jingle Workshop label that began life in 1957. OUTPUT: Based on catalogue numbers, twenty LPs were made, but very few of each custom pressed edition were issued as he tended to send out only to established clients in the Australian film / TV industry. Some LPs play the same on both sides; according to Bruce this was to keep one side for selection / audition purposes, the other for actual dubbing. STYLE: Standard mood music themes, pop, novelties, some drama, moog, electronics. MUSICIANS OF NOTE: Bruce Clarke, Dick Healey. SLEEVES: Bruce's magic musical pencil, drawn by renowned advertising agency Weatherhead and Stitt. All identical sleeves with pasted tracklisting on the reverse, some with hand typed labels.

IOTA

Action / Theme
Aaron Briggs
Bright, modern electronics.
BBC library sticker. (JT)

Atmospheric / Electronic
No artist credited
Bright, modern electronics.
BBC library sticker. (JT)

HISTORY: Obscure UK label set up in 1986. OUTPUT: Two LPs found. STYLE: A cross section of standard and experimental cues, lively, bright, electronic. MUSICIANS OF NOTE: Aaron Briggs, Raoul Phillips. SLEEVES: Simple but effective graphic logo. Colour changes on each volume.

JOLLY

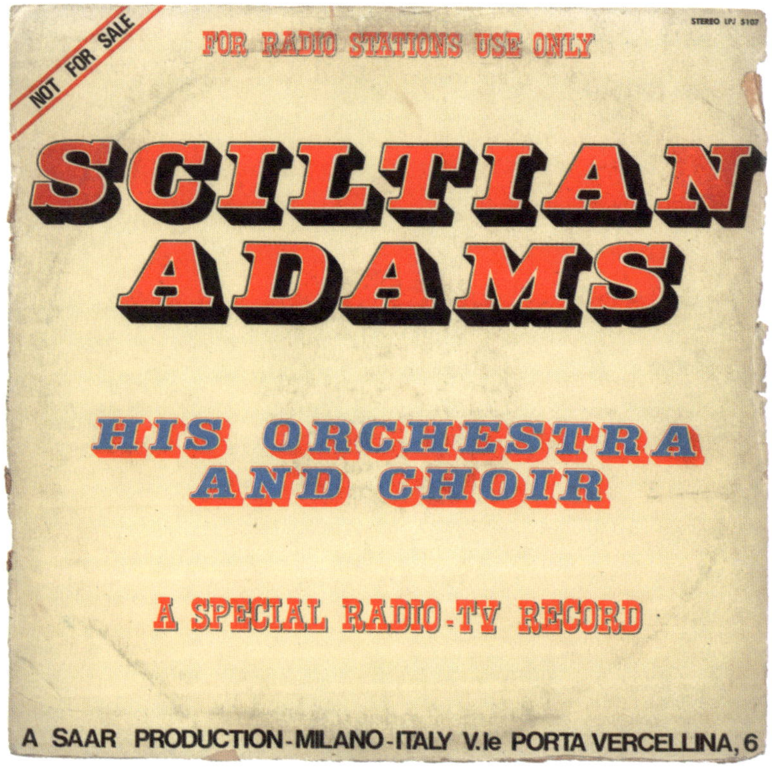

Feeling The Riot
Sciltian Adams
Various big band cues. (JK)

HISTORY: Large commercial Italian label based in Milan. Founded in 1958 by label owning legend Walter Guertler. OUTPUT: Large catalogue but very few records made for actual library usage. We have found just one. STYLE: Pretty groovy in an Italian fashion. MUSICIANS OF NOTE: Sciltian Adams. SLEEVES: A quiet riot of colour and unexpected fonts.

JOSEPH WEINBERGER
(JW MEDIA MUSIC)

Bob Downes' New Sounds
Percussive, exotic, eastern, avant-garde. (JT)

HISTORY: Legendary label, originating in Austria in 1884 as a publisher of musical theatre. UK company incorporated in 1937. Earliest recordings for Weinberger's Theme Music label dating from around 1956. Shortly afterwards it acquired the Inter Art Music company, who owned the Impress label. Later a third company and label was created, Background Music Publishers 'Audio' label, producing a further thirty LPs. OUTPUT: Very large number of LPs across 10" 78rpm and 12" 33rpm releases. STYLE: Everything from early avant-garde to standard easy mood music cues. MUSICIANS OF NOTE: Desmond Leslie, Sydney Dale, Bob Downes, Pete Thomas. SLEEVES: Early vinyl 12" releases with white and yellow block patterns, moving to plain light brown sleeves in the late 1970s. FAMOUS CUES: *Screen Test* theme, *9 O'Clock News* theme, *Plan 9 From Outer Space* incidentals.

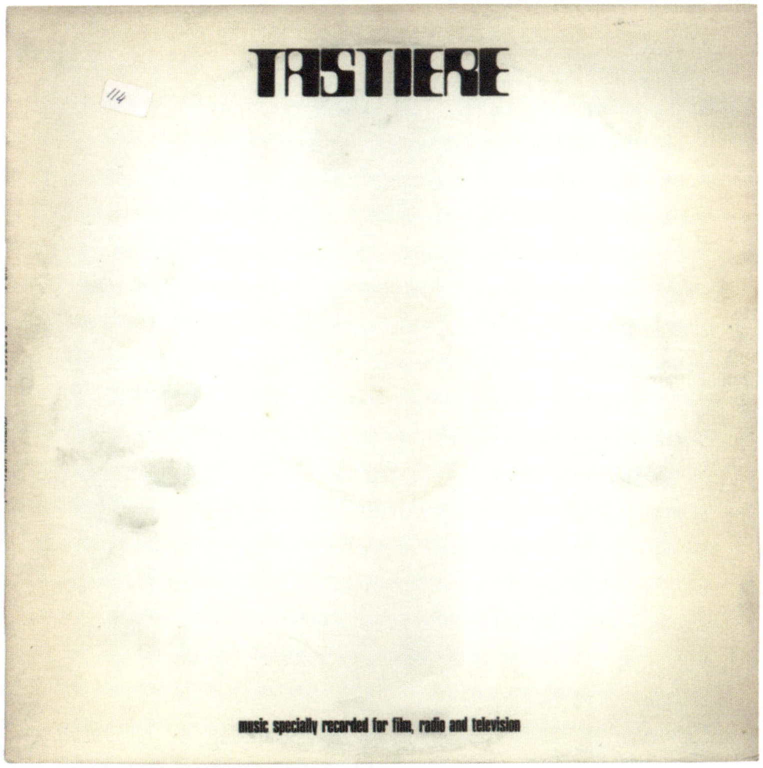

Tastiere
Paolo Ormi (legendary arranger)
Repetitive percussion and moog sounds. (JT)

Pentagramma
Nora Orlandi
Children's bossa and vocal cues .(JP)

HISTORY: Obscure Italian label, established in 1974. An experimental part of the RCA library catalogue. OUTPUT: Very small, only four releases traced. Rare LPs. STYLE: Jazz, electronics, percussion, world music sounds. MUSICIANS OF NOTE: Paolo Ormi, Nora Orlandi, The Barigozzi Group. SLEEVES: Mostly plain with simply typography. The first release uses stock photography.

Computer Sounds
Mornello / Panzutti etc
Standard electronic cues. (JT)

The Tropicals
Urubamba
Exotic, sought after jazz. (JK)

HISTORY: Italian music label operating in the 1970s and early 1980s. See also Music Scene. OUTPUT: A varied and interesting array of LPs – hard to find but around forty LPs manufactured. Some sublicensing. STYLE: From trad jazz to odd modern compositions. MUSICIANS OF NOTE: The Tropicals, The Holiday Mood Orchestra. SLEEVES: Several 'music stand' sleeves with changes in colour. Some other more unpredictable artwork based on stock photography and unusual but effective fonts.

KRONAL

Experience
Ezy Minus
Groovy jazz with wordless vocals. (JT)

HISTORY: Label started in Italy by Enzo Minuti in 1971. OUTPUT: Five LPs traced. All seem to be recordings by Minuti under his various Ezy Minus pseudonyms. STYLE: Progressive, easy, wordless jazz vocals. MUSICIANS OF NOTE: Ezy Minus. SLEEVES: Jazzy drawings and graphics by Minuti. A definitive house style.

KPM

KPM 1002
Syd Dale
Up tempo orchestral jazz, eccentric suspense. (SW)

HISTORY: Roots can be traced to Robert Keith, London 1780. Library recordings on 78rpm pressed from 1955. Green *1000 Series* began 1965, initiated by Robin Phillips. OUTPUT: Internationally renowned recordings, worldwide distribution, massive vinyl pressings and vast catalogue. MUSICIANS OF NOTE: Brian Bennett, John Cameron, Alan Parker, Keith Mansfield, Johnny Pearson, Francy Boland, Neil Ardley, Syd Dale, Ron Geesin. SLEEVES: Early 78s have plain card bags. Many of these recordings were repressed on the burnt orange sleeved 33rpm LPs. The *1000 Series* begins with the '11 block' sleeves, shortly afterwards changing to the classic olive green sleeves. From KPM 1260 sleeves all change to a more chaotic graphic and airbrushed 1980s style. FAMOUS CUES: *Mastermind*, *Captain Pugwash*, *Deep Throat* incidentals, *News At Ten*, *Wicker's World*.

The classic KPM 1000 Series.
Generic green sleeve. (JT)

Standard KPM Series, burnt orange sleeve.
Pre-1000 Series and repressed 78rpm recordings. (JT)

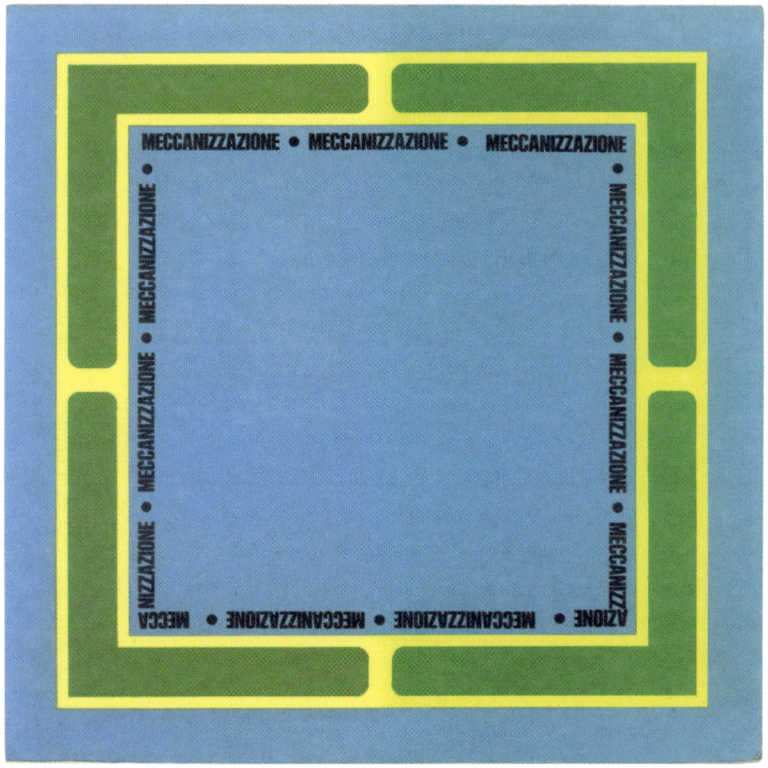

Percussioni In Crescendo
Giuliano Sorgini
Drums, Ziggurats. (JG)

Meccanizzazione
Oronzo De Filippi
Killer modal jazz. (JP)

HISTORY: Small library offshoot of the Italian Leonardi label. Operating for a short time from 1970. OUTPUT: Catalogue numbers suggest at least twenty-five LPs released, just over half have been traced. Rare and desirable albums. STYLE: Brilliant mix of progressive and odd sounds, jazz, rock, experimental compositions, often all on the same LP. MUSICIANS OF NOTE: Giuliano Sorgini, Remigio Ducros, Daniela Casa, Rino De Filippi. SLEEVES: Simple effective graphics. Some illustration, apparently sometimes drawn by the composers.

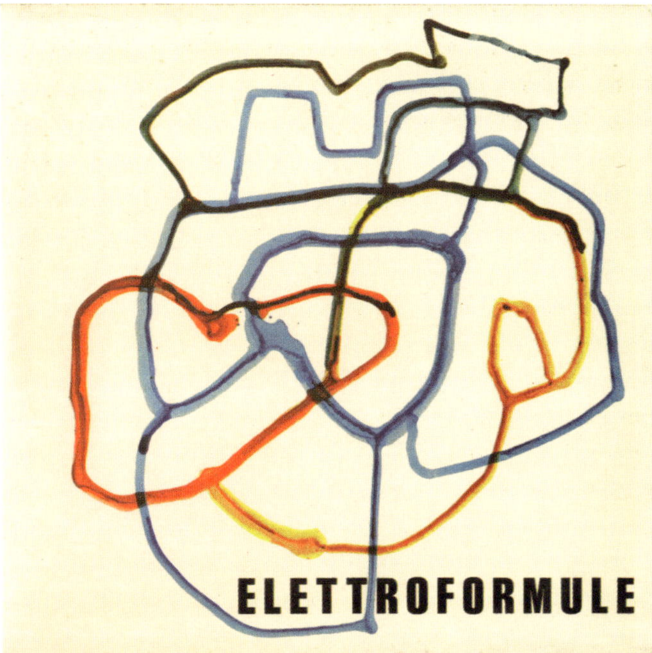

Elettroformule
Giuliano Sorgini
More important electronics. (S)

Vetrina Musicale
Alessandro Alessandroni
A fine carousel of sounds. (JT)

Musiche Per Un Telefilm
Renosto / Luciani
Beautiful sounds for TV. (S)

America Giovane No.2
Daniela Casa
American styled pop, rock and insanity. (JT)

LEONARDI

Telefilm
Simoncini
Exotic scores for TV usage. (JT)

Telefilm N.2
Giuliano Sorgini
Desirable progressives. (JP)

Telefilm N.2
Sorgini, Alessandroni
Folk, jazz, psychedelics, two LP set. (S)

HISTORY: Italian publishing house started in 1927 by Piero Leonardi. Moving into library music production in the 1960s. Father label of Grand Prix, Leo, Lupus, Metropole and Montecarlo. See also Cooper and Full. OUTPUT: Sporadic and unpredictable releases, catalogue numbers would suggest approximately twenty-five releases, but many are very rare, and some not yet traced or catalogued. Very desirable. STYLE: Interesting progressive styles, jazz and experimental releases. Some scores released as library music in the *Telefilm Series*. MUSICIANS OF NOTE: The Blue Sharks, Egisto Macchi, Giuliano Sorgini. SLEEVES: From simple typography to more illustrative artwork.

America Giovane
R. Ducros
Italy meets electric America. (S)

Carosello Musicale
Evasio Roncarati and Gino Mescoli
Various compositions. (JD)

Fauna Marina
Egisto Macchi
Incredible underwater experiments. (JT)

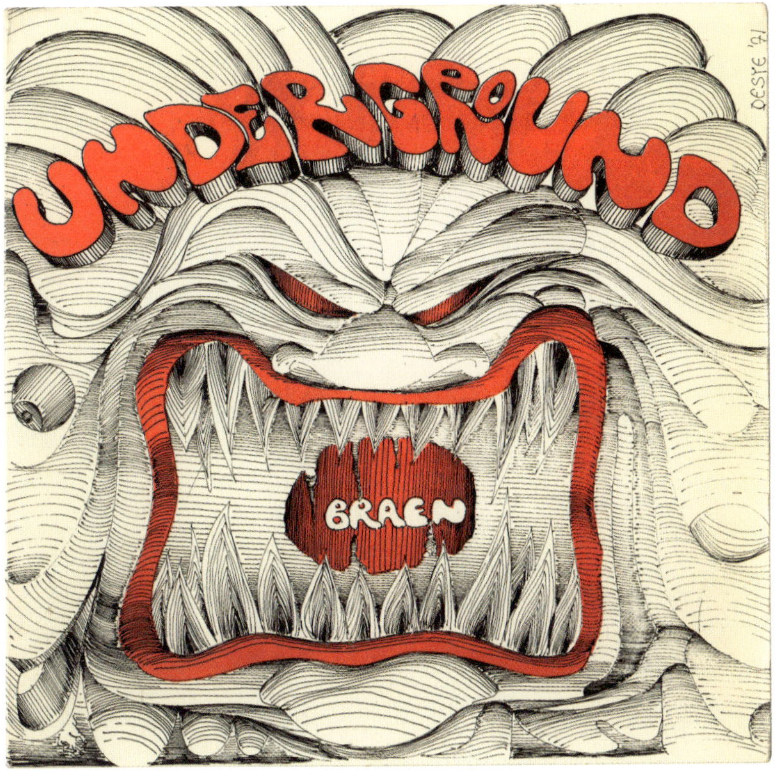

Underground
The Braen's Machine
Psychedelic rock. (S)

Guerra E Distruzione
Piero Umiliani
Dramatic sounds. two LP set. (S)

HISTORY: Composer Piero Umiliani's own Italian label. Started in Rome, late 1960s. Also affiliated with Sound Work Shop. Both library and soundtrack recordings issued. See also: Omicron, Telesound and Videovoice (and Ciak). OUTPUT: Prolific, possibly assisted by RCA distribution and pressing. Some international distribution via MP2000, sublicensing to St Germain Des Prés. STYLE: Filmic and thematic, experimental and electronics, jazzy concepts. High standard of musicianship. MUSICIANS OF NOTE: Piero Umiliani and his own pseudonyms, The Braen's Machine (Alessandroni, Rino De Filippi). SLEEVES: Various styles. Collage, photography and graphics.

Suspense
M. Zalla
Tense clever music. MP2000 distribution sticker. (JP)

To-Day's Sound
Umiliani and the Soundwork-Shoppers
MP2000 distribution sticker. (JG)

Gli Archi Raccontano
Piero Umiliani
Classical, pastoral themes. (JT)

Temi Ritmici E Dinamici
The Braen's Machine
Superb jazz and dramatics. (S)

Percussioni Ed Effetti Speciali
Piero Umiliani
Percussive double LP. (JT)

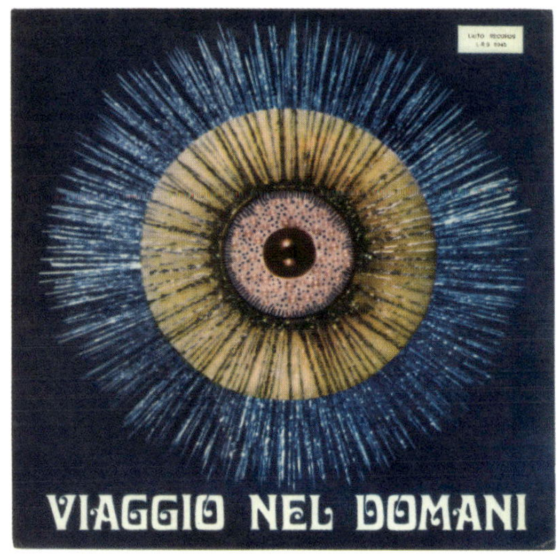

Viaggo Nel Domani
Ruscigan
Ambient and interesting electronics. (JP)

Informale n.3
Giuliano Sorgini
Very rare sonic experiments and drama. (S)

Immagini Moog
Paride Miglioli
Modern synthesis. (S)

HISTORY: Prolific label from Italy, c.1973. See also Leonardi. OUTPUT: High rate of LP production for international distribution. Original compositions and some sublicensing to Sonimage. STYLE: Broad range, some rare vocals in the *Telemusica Series*. MUSICIANS OF NOTE: Lesiman, Raskovich (Giuliano Sorgini), Ugo Fusco. SLEEVES: No generic feel, but consistently simple and effective artwork.

Telemusica No.6
Various artists
Easy, jazz. (JG)

Impressioni Musicali
Paride Miglioli
A diverse mixture of styles, from traditional to grotesque. (S)

Un Quartetto per Mario Gangi
Radici
Classical cues. (JT)

Colori Bozzetti E Miniature Musicali
Paride Miglioli
Experimental music. (S)

Psycheground
Ninety
Psychedelic sounds. (JG)

Italia Minima
Sordini and Casa
Various dramatics. (S)

MAJOR RECORDS

Volume 42
Bill Potts
From child's play to funeral marches. (JT)

HISTORY: American label started as part of the early and groundbreaking Thomas J. Valentino sound effects library. OUTPUT: Vast catalogue of original and sub-licensed recordings, across both 10″ 78rpm and 12″ 33rpm, pressing vinyl well into the 1980s. STYLE: All mood music and SFX needs catered for. MUSICIANS OF NOTE: Mario Nascimbene, Roger Roger, Thomas J. Valentino, Walter Murphy. SLEEVES: Some in plain sleeves, some in standard printed production 'disco bags'.

Tempo Di Naja
Remigio Ducros
Dramatic jazz. (JT)

Multifrequenze
Arawak
Experimental noise. (S)

HISTORY: Short lived Italian label. OUTPUT: Very few records traced, approximately twenty released. Little other information found. STYLE: Jazzy and experimental. MUSICIANS OF NOTE: Arawak. Paolo Casa. SLEEVES: Random and unpredictable mix of bold type, graphics and illustration.

MARCY MUSIC

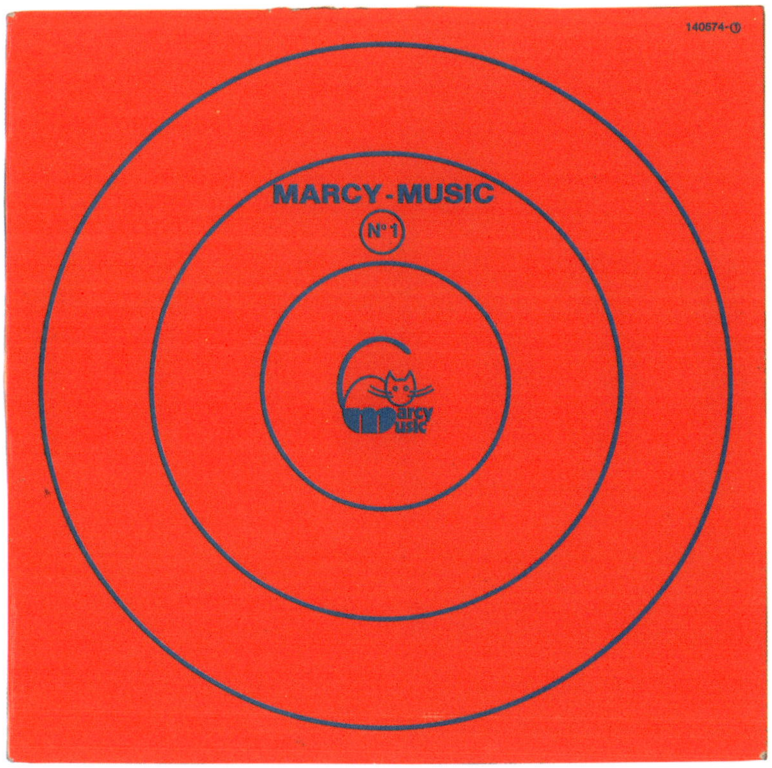

Timing No.1
Piget, Batailley, Ztepczak, Jourdain and Rolland
Dreamy fusion. (C)

HISTORY: French publishing house operating in the 1970s. OUTPUT: Just one library LP issued in 1974. No others found. STYLE: Experimental mood music from various composers. SLEEVES: Simple cat graphic.

MARIGNAN

The Top Twelve No.14
Mickey Nicolas
Up tempo jazz. (JG)

HISTORY: Small French label started in 1972. Possibly formed by musician René 'Mickey' Nicolas. OUTPUT: Up to fifteen albums traced. Poor distribution. All quite rare. STYLE: From classics to pop melodies and jazz. MUSICIANS OF NOTE: Yan Tregger, Mickey Nicolas. SLEEVES: Basic two colour with type variations.

Jazz Commento
Mario Nascimbene
Jazz score as moods. (JT)

HISTORY: Set up by film composing maestro Mario Nascimbene in Rome, 1968. OUTPUT: Catalogue suggests six LPs were produced, with film music and jazz repressed as library recordings. STYLE: Raw jazz, psychedelics, progressive compositions. MUSICIANS OF NOTE: Mario Nascimbene and Giuliano Sorgini. SLEEVES: LPs have identical black and white sleeves with 'sundial' graphic.

Selezione Di Orchestre
Ugo Fusco, Libero Tosoni etc
Fine and rare themes. (S)

Crociera Internazionale
M. Molino, Pelleus etc
Sounds for the jet set. Sonimage sticker. (S)

HISTORY: Italian label started in the early 1970s. Offshoot of the large Leonardi stable. OUTPUT: According to catalogue numbers, twenty-three LPs were issued. Rare and hard to find. Some sublicensing with Sonimage. STYLE: A jazz led catalogue, with experimental compositions. MUSICIANS OF NOTE: Stefano Torrosi, Santucci Scoppa Quintet. SLEEVES: A mixture of strong graphic and typographic styles.

VIDEO
MUSICA
N. 2

MATCHLESS SOUND

ITINERARIO
BEAT

MONDIOPHONE

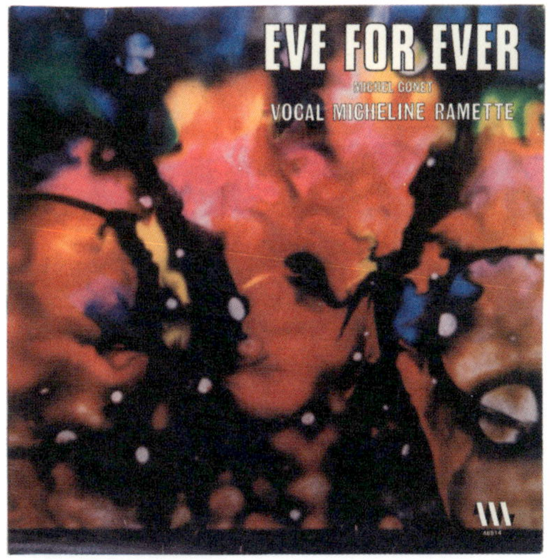

Wall Paper Music
Dave Sarkys
Instrumental and vocal sounds. (FM)

Actual
Georges Rodi
Psychedelic sounds. (JD)

Eve For Ever
Michel Gonet
Vocal jazz group sounds. (FM)

SO_4H_2
Michel Gonet
Modern moods. (JD)

Delirium Tremens
Camille Sauvage
Satan / perpetual motion / UFOs. (JT)

Profondeur 1000
Christian Zysset
Deep underwater jazz. (JT)

HISTORY: Large Paris based label, started in the early 1970s. Part of the Neuilly label. See also Crea Sound. OUTPUT: Large and varied catalogue, over sixty LPs pressed. Sublicensing worldwide. STYLE: All styles, genres and moods comprehensively covered. MUSICIANS OF NOTE: Michel Gonet, Janko Nilovic, Micheline Ramette. SLEEVES: Photographic manipulations.

Down In The City No.1
Franco Potenza
Urban jazz, small group. (SS)

Visioni
Various including Raskovich
Dramatic cues. (JT)

HISTORY: Rare Italian label from the late 1960s. Part of the Leonardi group. OUTPUT: Very small run of library LPs, some sublicensed. Less than ten LPs traced, but catalogue numbering suggest up to twenty LPs may have been produced. Rare and desirable. STYLE: Hip jazz, progressive and conceptual recordings. MUSICIANS OF NOTE: Giuliano Sorgini. A.R. Luciani, Ugo Fusco. SLEEVES: Typography and illustration with no distinct style.

L'Acqua N.1
Antonino Riccardo Luciani
Underwater music. (JT)

L'Acqua N.2
Antonino Riccardo Luciani
More fine underwater music. (JP)

MONTPARNASSE 2000
(MP2000)

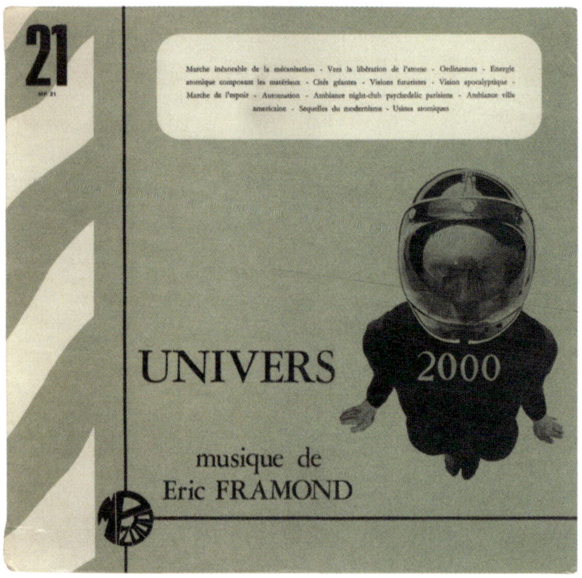

96. **Music the food of life**
The Jack Dieval's Sextet
Modern jazz themes. (JM)

21. **Univers 2000**
Eric Framond
Satan meets jazz. (C)

14. **Delirius Music**
Jean Jacques Robert and Jean Michel Guise
Exotic and erotic jazz. (MK)

HISTORY: One of the great, prolific labels from Paris, established as a music label but moved into library music from 1968 until the mid-1970s. Label started by Andre Farry, assisted by Louis Delacour (aka Pepe Luis). Small offshoot label called St Germain Des Prés. OUTPUT: Large and consistent, regular pressing and repressings. Good international distribution. Over one hundred and thirty LPs produced. MUSICIANS OF NOTE: Daniel White, Janko Nilovic, Eric Framond. SLEEVES: Highly distinctive. Unique flag design which continues on spine. Early releases used illustrations and photography, these changed to block colours and simple type for represses.

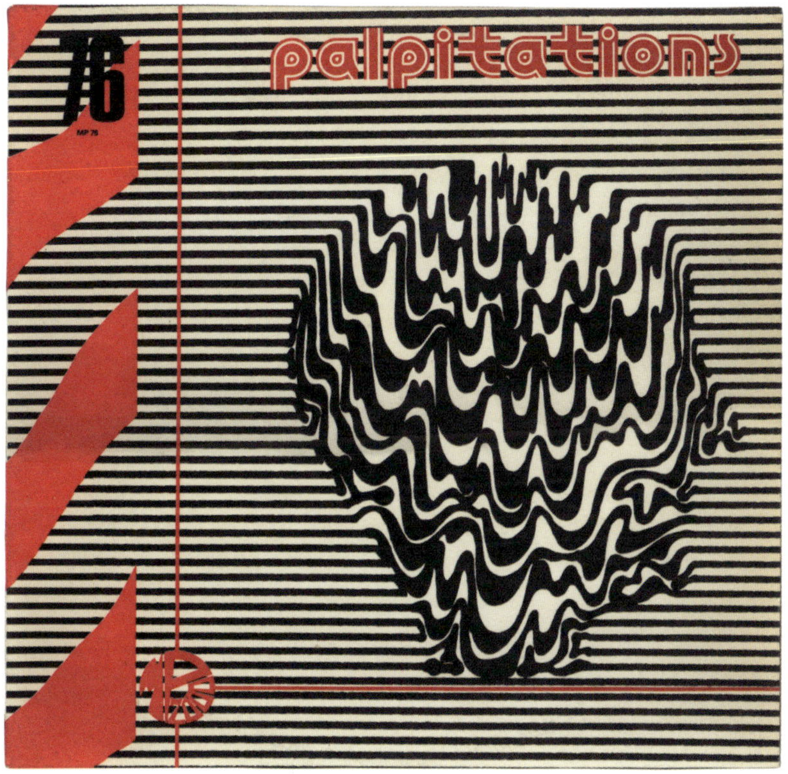

76. **Palpitations**
Eric Framond
Twisted jazz themes. (JG)

40. **Stylissimo**
Camille Sauvage and Jerry Mengo
Electronic madness. (LV)

Vocal Impressions
Janko Nilovic and Dave Sucky
Fine scatty jazz and improvisation. (JT)

84. **Un Homme Dans l'Univers**
Janko Nilovic
Keyboard led easy listening. (C)

6. **Psyc' Impressions**
Janko Nilovic and Dave Sucky
Deranged, guitar led psychedelia. (C)

46. **Musique A Show**
Eric Framond
Classical / progressive with heavy percussion. (C)

33. **Fantasmagories**
Camille Sauvage
Horror themes, percussive abstract fusion. (C)

68. **Puzzle** Actualities Series
Eric Framond
Pop / sports. (JM)

25. **Moog Sensations**
J. J. Perry and P. Prilly
Fast boogie to slow foxtrot, in moog. (JM)

13. **Monologue Pour**
Daniel J. White
Solo instruments. (JT)

122. **Rêve Abyssal**
Gaston Borreani
Into the watery abyss. (JT)

124. **Régénération**
Roger Davy
Cosmic electronics. (JT)

67. **16e – 18e**
Robert Irancy and Bernard Andres
Period music, solo instrument compositions. (JT)

91. **Sound**
Jean-Pierre Decerf / Marc Saclays etc
Moody electronics. (JT)

75. **Ben The Big One**
Ronnie Hazlehurst
The London day in jazz and twaddles. (JT)

MOZART EDITION

LP031
The Perry / Gardner Orchestra
Various light orchestrals including *Sailing By*. (JT)

HISTORY: Large British label, established in the 1950s to produce and publish classical and light orchestral recordings for use in TV, radio and film. One of the earliest libraries to record in stereo. OUTPUT: Large and slightly international catalogue of over one hundred LPs, with music from a variety of sources and a wide range of composers. STYLE: Mainly light orchestral and classical, with some novelty and comedy recordings. MUSICIANS OF NOTE: Ronald Binge, Alan Langford, David Lyon, 'Fabor', Giampiero Boneschi. SLEEVES: Simple orange sleeve with logo, back covers are blank except for a small black logo and square; the LPs tracklisting, cat number and title is then pasted in the blank square. FAMOUS CUES: *Sailing By* (used for the BBC Radio 4 Shipping Forecast).

MUSAX

Sequencer
Joachim Sherylee
Electronic industrials. (JT)

019
Paul Baile
Cold blooded contemporary sounds. (JT)

HISTORY: French label started in the late 1970s, after the demise of the IM (L'Illustration Musicale) label. Run by Jacky Giordano. OUTPUT: Small series of LPs. STYLE: Electronic, lively, dramatic. MUSICIANS OF NOTE: Bernard Fevre, Camille Sauvage, Roger Roger, Nino Nardini. SLEEVES: Early editions have printed disco bag with small relevant illustration around the centre hole. Later issues have illustrative / typographic sleeves.

No 1
Daniel White
Descriptive dabblings. (JT)

HISTORY: Obscure label from France in the late 1960s. OUTPUT: Only one LP found to date. STYLE: Easy, experimental. MUSICIANS OF NOTE: Daniel White. SLEEVES: Two colour sleeve with simple repetitive photography.

MUSICAL TOUCH SOUND

Catchy
Yan Tregger
Disco moods. Artwork by Oklay. (S)

Dreamland
Arsen Gedik
Electronic novelties and ambience. (JT)

HISTORY: Small label started in 1976, based in Paris. Possibly owned by Yan Tregger. OUTPUT: Fifteen LPs issued over a four year period. STYLE: Electronics with a lively feel, moving into disco and fantasy cues. SLEEVES: Bizarre illustration and graphics.

MUSIC SCENE

Unusual Beat Sounds Fantasy
Giampiero Boneschi
Dance, electronic and moody themes.
TRF distribution sticker. (LV)

HISTORY: Prolific Italian library label, c.1970. Part of the Jump publishing group. OUTPUT: Large and impressive, one hundred and thirty-seven LPs across two catalogues. Some international licensing. STYLE: A mixture of classic and mood music cues and some experimental electronics. MUSICIANS OF NOTE: Carlo Savina, Barigozzi, Oscar Rocchi, Boneschi, Minus Vocal Group. SLEEVES: MS / MSE Series have the clover leaf sleeves printed in shades of green and red. For the TRF series, anything goes.

MUSIKVERLAG OCTAVE

Musik Mosaik Volume 3
Bottcher and Kuhn
Musical experiments. (JD)

HISTORY: German label based in Hamburg, mid to late 1970s. OUTPUT: Six library LPs traced. Now rare. STYLE: Jazz based, experimentals. MUSICIANS OF NOTE: Bob Elger, Egisto Macchi. SLEEVES: Simple, sparse and numbered graphics.

MUSIQUE CINÉMA TÉLÉVISION
(M.C.T.)

105 **New-Music**
André Ceccarelli and friends
Modern versatile sounds. (JT)

HISTORY: Small label from Paris. Started in the 1980s and with some publishing connections with Patchwork. OUTPUT: A handful of LPs issued, some appearing on the Patchwork label. STYLE: Modern, electronic. MUSICIANS OF NOTE: Teddy Lasry, Andre Ceccarelli, Bernard Arcadio, Domonique Guiot. SLEEVES: Distinctive two box outline / one photo style sleeves.

MUSIQUE POUR L'IMAGE

MPI. No.6. **Jazz Mobile**
Henri Renaud, Robert Hermel, Martial Solal
Fine jazz.
Sleeve by Robert J. Hilton. (JH)

MPI. No.5. **Espace Et Actualité**
Patrice Sciortino, Claude Vasori, François Bayle
Sleeve by Robert J. Hilton. (JH)

MPI. No.26. **Guitares Rythmes Et Guitares**
Roger Davey
1970. Sleeve by Robert J. Hilton. (JH)

HISTORY: Important Paris based label, started by pianist and jazz composer Robert Viger. Began issuing 10" recordings c.1968, changing to 12" LPs after twenty issues. OUTPUT: Fifty-five LPs issued across 10" and 12". Rare and desirable recordings. STYLE: A complete range from jazz dramatics to experimental and children's music. MUSICIANS OF NOTE: Geminiani, Vladimir Cosma, Claude Vasori, Martial Solal. SLEEVES: Stunning black and white graphics and photography, collages also. Most sleeves by Robert J. Hilton. Later LPs feature colour and photography.

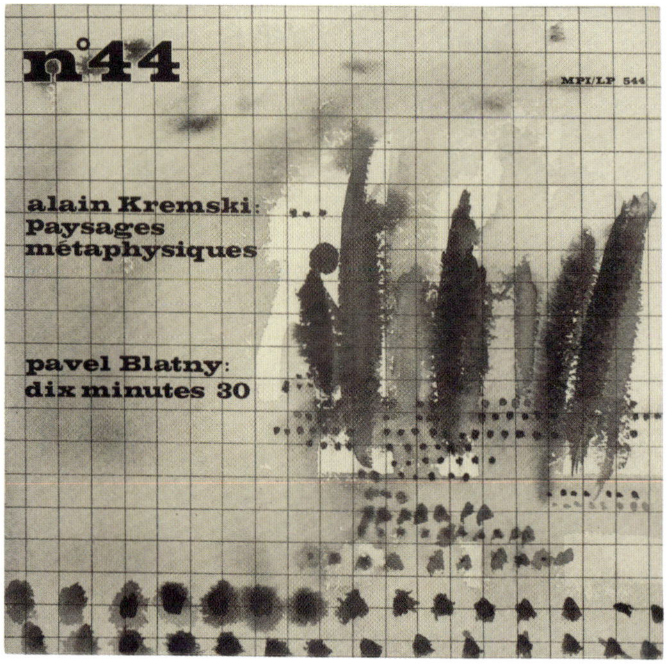

MPI. No.44. **Paysages Métaphysiques**
Alain Kremski
Strange musical pulsations. (JT)

MPI. No.33. **Sons Nouveaux Pour Images Contemporaines**
Roger Davey
Various exotic, jazz and progressive themes. (JT)

MPI. No.29. **Images En Movement**
Claude Vasori
Includes *Drug Pop*. Sleeve by Didier La Mache. (JG)

MPI. No.39. **Harlem Pop Trotters**
J. B. Raiteux
Improvised folk and more. (S)

MPI. No.35. **Voyage Extraordinaire**
Vincent Geminiani
Art meets pop, jazz and percussion. (FM)

MPI. No.38. **Infini**
Fabio Fabor, Armando Sciascia
Italian experiments. (SS)

MPI. No.24. **Jazz Pour L'Action**
Richard Eldwyn
Fast and fine jazz themes. (JG)

Quick Silver
Roger Simon
Rapid jazz. (JT)

MPI. No.36. **Cocktail D'Images**
Claude Vasori
Vibrant, jazzy listening. (JG)

MPI. No.27. **Ultra Pop Op**
Vladimir Cosma
Sleeve by Robert Planet. (JG)

MPI. No.22. **Action**
Martial Solal
Fine jazz for action. (JT)

MPI. No.34. **Enfance**
Vladimir Cosma
Electro-medieval sounds. (JT)

MPI. No.2. **Action Charme Espace**
Claude Vasori
All jazz sounds. (JG)

MPI. No.23. **Images De L'Enfance**
Robert Viger, Jean Naty etc
Naïve music. (JT)

Tema: Amore
Rino De Filippi
Sounds of modern love. (JT)

Supermarket
Raskovich etc
Modern industrials. (JT)

HISTORY: Tiny Italian label, based in Milan, started in the late 1960s. OUTPUT: Less than ten LPs traced (catalogue numbers start at 019) with international distribution via Eurobeat. Possibly some sublicensing, but rare nonetheless. STYLE: Jazzy, light orchestral, progressive, electronic. MUSICIANS OF NOTE: Rino De Filippi, Paolo Renosto, Ray Green, Raskovich. SLEEVES: The set of *Supermarket* LPs have the same stock photo and type. Others have individual art and graphics.

NELSON

I Marc 4
Issued on Silver Music
Super cool jazz directions. (MK)

HISTORY: Italian label, set up in 1970, issuing the work of I Marc 4. OUTPUT: Thirteen original albums were issued up until 1971. Two I Marc 4 LPs with identical artwork to the Nelson LPs were issued on the 'Silver Music' label. We can only assume these labels are the same. STYLE: Experimental and exciting jazz music for synchronisation. MUSICIANS OF NOTE: I Marc 4. SLEEVES: Most issues follow the standard design with tracklisting panel on the right, and block colour on the left.

NEREIDE

La Natura E L'Uomo
Alessandro Alessandroni
Gentle, groovy and odd sounds. (S)

HISTORY: Small Italian label. OUTPUT: Just one LP traced. We believe this label is directly related to Cenacolo, and Rhombus (as well as Cardium, Chic, Musical, Spring and Weekend), possibly all overseen by Alessandroni, Tommasi and their associates, and started by publisher Maria Stecchetti. STYLE: Light, easy, unusual. MUSICIANS OF NOTE: Alessandro Alessandroni, Amedeo Tommasi. SLEEVES: One colour with simple title, as with all the other labels mentioned.

Musique En Couleurs
Alan Blackwell
Accomplished scat jazz. (JT)

HISTORY: Paris based label founded by Louis Delacour. International distribution under the Creasound label. See also Mondiophone. OUTPUT: Mid-sized catalogue of at least forty releases on both 10" and 12". STYLE: Electronics, easy listening, experimental and jazz. MUSICIANS OF NOTE: Roger Roger, Nino Nardini, Janko Nilovic. SLEEVES: Early sleeves use simple typography. Later sleeves show a more illustrative style, some with photography. Many have Creasound stickers or re-badging.

Sports Plein Air
Roger Roger
Creasound licensing sticker over Neuilly logo. (SS)

Jungle Obssession
Nino Nardini and Roger Roger
Killer exotics. (FM)

Musique Idiote
Roger Roger
Insane electronics. (LO)

Musique Pour Le Futur
Nino Nardini
Visionary electronics. (JD)

NEW BINGO

Shake With Care
The Cotton Flocks
Fluffy jazz. MP2000 sticker. (SG)

HISTORY: Based in Rome. Part of the Duse record company, who in turn are part of the larger Beat label. See also Pentaphon, Pony and Gemini. OUTPUT: All produced around 1975, very few LPs were made, we have traced seven. Some distribution by MP2000. STYLE: Light jazz, easy listening, experimental. MUSICIANS OF NOTE: Phil Webster, The Cotton Flocks. SLEEVES: All have the same design, drawn by Cavallaro.

NEW SOUTHERN LIBRARY

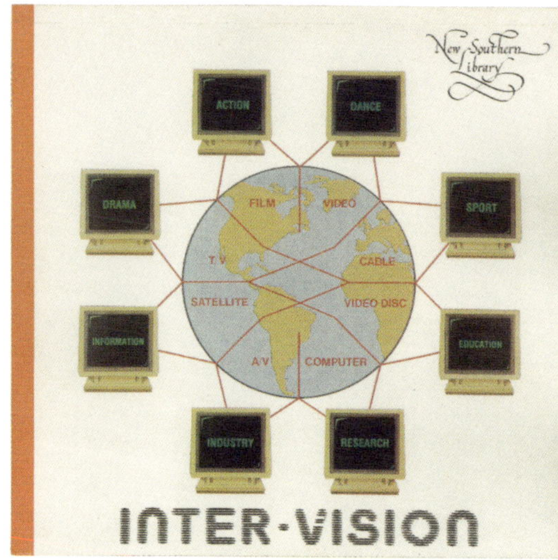

Inter-Vision
James Asher
Contemporary sequenced electronics. (JT)

Time Cycle
James Asher
A festival of 1980s synthesis. (JP)

HISTORY: Started in 1981, this was a modern associated label for Southern, a label that had stopped pressing new music in 1974. OUTPUT: Nineteen LPs over a seven year period. STYLE: Experimental, electronic, modern, corporate, industrial. MUSICIANS OF NOTE: James Asher, Alan Hawkshaw, Duncan Lamont. SLEEVES: Early sleeves have the Southern scroll logo and font on simple white backgrounds. Later issues have bolder and more experimental graphics.

NEW TAPE

Tropical
Santucci Scoppa
Exotic jazz and space themes. (CG)

HISTORY: Italian label , early 1970s, linked to RCA Italy. OUTPUT: Four LPs found, two others may exist. Some seem to be related to sessions on other rare library labels. STYLE: Jazz, musical experiments. MUSICIANS OF NOTE: Santucci Scoppa, Lesiman, Romolo Grano. SLEEVES: The oversized New Tape logo with changes in colour and repeated LP title.

NIKE

Trasparenze
Bruno Battisti D'Amario
Some darkish bossas. (JT)

Tensioni
Bruno Battisti D'Amario
Hard and percussive drama cues. (JT)

HISTORY: Italian label started 1973, possibly owned by musician Bruno Battisti D'Amario. OUTPUT: Very small, just five albums. STYLE: Dramatic industrial cues, tension, some folk. MUSICIANS OF NOTE: Bruno Battisti D'Amario, Edda Dell'Orso, Franco Goldani. SLEEVES: Nike square and goddess, changes in numbers, title and colour for each release.

NUOVA IDEA

Voci E Suoni
Fernando Marucci
Modern classical, odd baroque. (S)

HISTORY: Italian label dating from the early 1970s, part of the large Flipper music house. OUTPUT: Small catalogue (possibly only ten LPs) of interesting library recordings. Sought after. STYLE: Progressive, jazzy, experimental, easy. MUSICIANS OF NOTE: Ugo Busoni, Paolo Ferrara, Corvasce. SLEEVES: Early sleeves use same stock image as Picci LPs. Later LPs use same simple graphics as Flower and Octopus.

OAK

Synthesized Sounds
Basil Tait
Interesting 1980s bridges, stings and concepts. (JT)

HISTORY: Little known British label from the 1980s. Based in Pinner, Middlesex. Maybe started by Basil Tait, at his home. OUTPUT: Hard to discover, few references can be found. Catalogue numbers would suggest at least twelve, but to date we have found just one LP. STYLE: Electronics. MUSICIANS OF NOTE: Basil Tait. SLEEVES: Grid with appropriate futuristic font.

Telegiornale Octopus 7
Atmo (aka Amedeo Tommasi)
Jazz and psychedelia. (JT)

Clouds
Lino and Castiglione
Funky jazz fusion. (SS)

HISTORY: Independent Italian label based in Rome, founded in 1970. Originally part of the Canopo group which was absorbed in the mid-1970s by the larger Flipper music house. OUTPUT: Low number of pressings, possibly just twenty LPs. STYLE: Progressive and interesting, jazz, folk, experimental. MUSICIANS OF NOTE: Alessandro Alessandroni, Stefan Grossman. SLEEVES: Early issues have a pink octopus on the sleeve; this changed to graphic typography in later issues.

OLYMPO

Impacto
The Bigroup
Rock and funk.
Originally issued as Big Hammer on the Peer label. (S)

HISTORY: Obscure Spanish pop label started in 1970, ended in 1984. OUTPUT: Just two library LPs found. STYLE: Mainly rock and funk dramatics. MUSICIANS OF NOTE: Barrie Forgie and Big Hammer. SLEEVES: Bold graphics.

OMICRON

Relax
Herbana
Fine, gentle sounds. (JK)

HISTORY: Synchronisation label started by Piero Umiliani in 1964 to safeguard and publish his own music (probably named after a film score he wrote in 1963). This grows into several other labels (from 1967 onwards), all issuing music by Umiliani under his many pseudonyms (including Moggi, Rovi, Tusco). See also Liuto, Sound Work Shop, Telesound and Videovoice (and Ciak). OUTPUT: Approximately thirty-seven LP releases. Rare and desirable. STYLE: Experimental, easy, filmic. MUSICIANS OF NOTE: Piero Umiliani under various pseudonyms. SLEEVES: Graphic with photography, illustration and occasional nudity.

Synthi Time
Piero Umiliani
VCS3 games. (JT)

Il Mondo Dei Romani
Piero Umiliani
Modern sounds masquerading as old. (S)

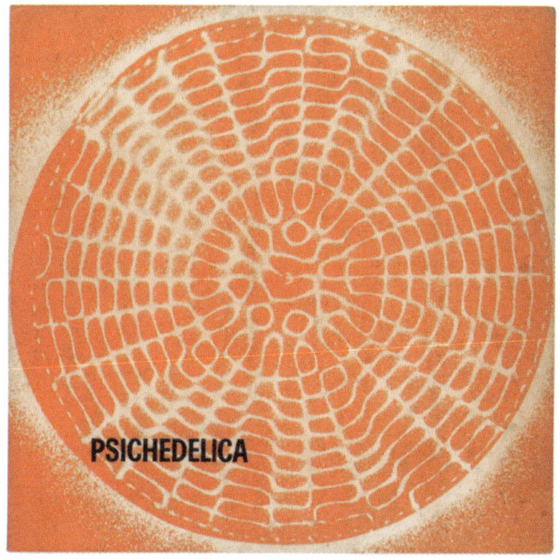

Psichedelica Sonorisation Series
Piero Umiliani
Very rare documentary jazz and psychedelics. (JS)

Effetti Musicali Sonorisation Series
Piero Umiliani
Experimental ambient electronics. (JT)

Gli Italiani E L'Industria
Piero Umiliani
Rare early industrial sounds. (JS)

Tra Scienze E Fantascienza
Moggi
Futuristic sounds for musical minions. (JT)

OMNIMUSIC

OM1 **Prime Time**
D. McAllister / J. Alter / M. Gaide
Late 1970s commercial music. (JT)

HISTORY: American library label set up in 1980 by composer Douglas Wood. OUTPUT: Medium sized catalogue by the mid-1980s, with over fifty LPs issued. Some distribution via Studio G in the UK and Europe. STYLE: Classic test card and Ceefax style sounds. Quite adventurous. MUSICIANS OF NOTE: Douglas Wood. SLEEVES: Generic white sleeve with simple black logo graphic, early editions have sleeve of thick card with a sheet pasted on the front, shown here. Many have Omni music score inserts as well as inner sleeves. FAMOUS CUES: *Drag Racer* – BBC Snooker theme.

ORLY

Mr. Diabolicus / Mr. Mysterious
Kaleidoscope No.13.
Fabio Fabor
Hectic electronics from the Kaleidoscope Series. (JT)

HISTORY: Paris based label, c.1969. OUTPUT: Average sized catalogue with approximately twenty LPs and some experimental 7″ records. Some sublicensing with Cenacolo. STYLE: Original French music and licensed experimentals from Italy. MUSICIANS OF NOTE: Giampiero Boneschi, Fabio Fabor. SLEEVES: Generic two colour bordered sleeve. Also issued a long series of spin painting sleeves.

ORRERY RECORD

Explosive
Arawak
Powerful electronic concepts. (S)

HISTORY: Unusual and small library company from Italy, set up in the mid-1970s. OUTPUT: Just three LPs located to date. STYLE: Pastoral to progressive. MUSICIANS OF NOTE: Arawak (Luciano Simoncini). SLEEVES: No distinct style – a mixture of odd fonts, visuals and some graph paper.

OTTER

Background Music N.1
Raskovich
Rare cosmic compositions. (S)

HISTORY: Small mid-1970s Italian label. OUTPUT: Very few LPs released. Less than ten. STYLE: Progressive, with American soul leanings. MUSICIANS OF NOTE: Raskovich, Paolo Casa. SLEEVES: No set style, a mixture of heavy graphics, unusual illustrations and typography. The N.1 sleeve shown here appears across other libraries in different colourways, including Lupus.

4+1
The Yellow Sharks
Hip easy and jazz. (MK)

Informale N.4
Raskovich
Superb dramatics. (S)

HISTORY: Small Italian label set up in the early 1970s. OUTPUT: Twenty-six LPs traced to date. All rare and desirable, but not all for synchronisation. STYLE: Abstract, avant-garde, jazzy, experimental. MUSICIANS OF NOTE: Braen, Raskovich, Daniela Casa, The Yellow Sharks. SLEEVES: No house style, a mixture of odd fonts, strange illustrations and bold graphics.

PARRY MUSIC

Journey Into Space
Artus and Kass
Drama with electronics and synthesisers. (JD)

Vernissage N.2
Daniela Casa
Rare avant-garde recordings. (JP)

Diplomazia In Armi
Domenico Guacerro
Free experimentals. (JP)

HISTORY: Founded in Canada in 1974 by John Parry and Chris Stone. OUTPUT: Very large, over one hundred and seventy LPs produced up until 1987. Some European distribution via Studio G. STYLE: Mainly electronic and experimental, with a contemporary feel. MUSICIANS OF NOTE: Johnny Hawksworth, Roger Roger. SLEEVES: The first one hundred and fifty-six LPs have the maple leaf design with simple changes in font and title.

34. **Energie**
Claude Perraudin
Post disco conceptual electronics. (JT)

13.
Marc Chantereau / Delaporte
More electronics. (JD)

HISTORY: Mid-1970s Paris based label. OUTPUT: Very large catalogue with over eighty LPs made. Some collaborations with Musique Cinéma Télévision (M.C.T.) STYLE: Mainly electronic, conceptual and modern. MUSICIANS OF NOTE: Teddy Lasry, Eric Demarsan, Guy Boulanger, Vladimir Cosma. SLEEVES: The first seventy-five LPs all have the op art square designs in bold colourways.

PEER INTERNATIONAL LIBRARY LIMITED
(PILL)

Point Blank
Dorothy Lapelle
Panther formed for this recording only. (S)

Flip Top
Barrie Moore Combo
Various jazz moods. (MG)

HISTORY: Classic London label based in Denmark Street. Started c.1968. Affiliated with Southern, many titles appear across both labels. OUTPUT: Forty-four LPs pressed, but in small numbers. Now scarce. STYLE: Jazz to classics, with a good range of electronics and progressive rock. MUSICIANS OF NOTE: Sven Libaek, Johnny Scott and the Scottmen, Nino Nardini. SLEEVES: Wide ranging styles, using photography and graphics. Distinctive and dynamic.

Inter-Relation
Johnny Scott and his Scottmen
Good jazz. 1970. (S)

Solar Flares
Sven Libaek and his Orchestra
Space age vibey jazz. (S)

Workforce Percussion Unit
Dramatic industrials.
Southern Library pressing. (S)

Gemini The Barrie Moore Combo
Anthony Mawer
Progressive easy listening. (SS)

Scoop
John Fiddy, Brain Dee, Clive Hicks
Dramatic and sporting themes. (S)

Sweet Surprise
Various artists
Classical strings. (JT)

Electric Bazaar
Anthony King
Electronics, toys, cats and storms. (S)

No Waiting
Peter Dennis Orchestra
Light moods. (SS)

Confrontation
Frank Sterling Big Band
Large orchestrals. (SS)

Five Plus Four
Powerhouse
Al Newman plays jazz. (S)

Lost Star
Memo
Includes *Filigree Funk*. 1978. (JM)

Soul of a City
Leonhardt and his Orchestra
Urban sounds. (SS)

Sun-Seeker
David Johnson
Guitar action. (MG)

Mind Bender
Nino Nardini, Roger Roger, Forgie and Anthony Mawer
Legendary progressive pop sounds by Stringtronics. (MG)

Hangover
Wolfgang Schlüter Combo
European jazz fusion. Artwork by Jack Mooring. (JT)

String Scene
Anthony Mawer Orchestra
Light orchestral and Latin moods. 1970. (JM)

My Thing
Sven Libaek
Pop / jazz. Includes *Misty Canyon*. (JT)

Earth Shaker
Midas Touch
Romance / disco / marches. (S)

PEGASO

Ho Incontrato Un'Ombra
Romolo Grano
Great soundtrack jazz / soul. (JT)

HISTORY: Another Italian offshoot of RCA. LPs pressed from 1971 onwards. OUTPUT: Primarily a soundtrack label, but a few library LPs and rare unreleased soundtracks issued just for synchronisation. Less than ten LPs pressed. Rare. Desirable. STYLE: Jazz, soul, funk, experimental, drama. MUSICIANS OF NOTE: Berto Pisano, Romolo Grano. SLEEVES: Often plain white with simple type.

PENTAPHON

Descrittivi
Oronzo De Filippi
Solo piano, primitive atmospheres. (JT)

HISTORY: Seemingly non-commercial library offshoot of Beat Records. Started c.1969. See also Gemini, Pony and New Bingo. OUTPUT: A few LPs issued using Beat composers and artwork. Several standard music LPs re-badged and sent out for synchronisation. STYLE: Spaghetti sounds, harmonica, jazz. Pastoral cues. Light classical. MUSICIANS OF NOTE: Mario Bertolazzi, Sol Kaplan. SLEEVES: 'Pearl' sleeves indentical to some in Beat library series.

PHOTOPLAY Q

Q Photoplay 13 Series
Ronnie Hazlehurst
Various easy cues. (S)

HISTORY: Small London label based in St John's Wood. Probably started and owned by Philip Green, ex house arranger at Decca. OUTPUT: Small but well formed library, fourteen LPs traced. STYLE: Easy listening, big band, jazz quartets, light modern pop. MUSICIANS OF NOTE: Ronnie Hazlehurst, Philip Green. SLEEVES: There are two series of LPs (Q12 and Q13), with purple or red sleeves, all with the large 'Q' graphic.

PICCI

The Fast Machine
Oscar Lindok
Quirky, progressive, funky, electronic. (S)

HISTORY: Set up in 1972 by composer Pino Cassia, this small Italian progressive label lasted just a couple of years. See also Champion. OUTPUT: Very small, less than fifteen LPs. STYLE: Amazing jazz in amongst fine dramatics and industrials. MUSICIANS OF NOTE: Oscar Lindok, Vasco, some pseudonyms. SLEEVES: Some spin painting, some stock photography (as also seen in the Nuova Idea catalogue).

PINCIANA

Teleradiosonory
Vassili Kojukarov
Interesting mood music. (S)

Complesso I Panamera – Al Night Club
Franco Bonfanti, Ernesto Fontana, Vipar etc
Nocturnal sounds, bossa nova. (JK)

Dodici Rose Rosse
Walter Rizzati
Groovy sounds and ideas. (JK)

HISTORY: Part of the Dany Records imprint. Active in Italy throughout the mid-1970s. OUTPUT: Very few LPs traced, catalogue numbers would suggest at least eight produced. Quite rare. STYLE: Light industrials to Latin jazz. MUSICIANS OF NOTE: Walter Rizzati, Franco Bonfanti, Vassili Kojukarov. SLEEVES: Strong and simple graphic style, many with single colour and circle, sometimes with title / artist written in the circle, some with no title at all.

Nightpiece
Stefano Busa
Bossas, jazz, trouble. (JT)

Pellicano, Sottofondi Musicali
George Jodriz, Walcover
Some very average compositions. (JT)

HISTORY: Tiny label set up in Rome, c.1978. OUTPUT: Just two library LPs traced to date. STYLE: Standard industrials. MUSICIANS OF NOTE: Stefano Busa, George Jodriz. SLEEVES: Slightly odd two colour graphics, and sometimes a pelican.

PLAYPHONE

Percussioni
Peymont
Various rare percussive ideas. (S)

HISTORY: Very small label set up in Rome, c.1971. OUTPUT: Only three library LPs found to date. STYLE: Percussion, some jazz. MUSICIANS OF NOTE: Luciano Simoncini. SLEEVES: Paired back typography. Some appropriate illustration.

PM
(PEGGY MONCLAIR)

Music For Show Volume 4
No artists named.
Brazilian themes and tangos. (LV)

HISTORY: Early 1970s label from Paris. OUTPUT: Four LPs traced. STYLE: Pop to jazz, with heavy focus on popular international rhythms. MUSICIANS OF NOTE: Gérard Cohen. SLEEVES: Painted representations of a car through a porthole.

Due Volti: Una Musica
Various artists including Voodoo
Experimental cues. (JT)

Addio Juna
Walter Rizzati
Farewell music. (JT)

Franco Chiari E Il Suo Complesso
Franco Chiari
Shakes, samba, clowns. (JT)

HISTORY: Rome based label from c.1974, affiliated with the larger Beat label. See also Beat, Duse, New Bingo, Pentaphon, Gemini. OUTPUT: Small and unpredictable, ten LPs have been found. STYLE: From classical cues to jazz. MUSICIANS OF NOTE: Mario Molino, Alessandroni, Bonfanti. SLEEVES: Diverse designs including illustration, photography and typography. No house style but the same LPs can be found in any one of the three styles shown.

POPULAR DISC

Delta Sound
J. C. Pierric
Jazz, funk and vocal harmonies. (JG)

HISTORY: Label based in Bezons, north west of Paris. OUTPUT: Very limited, rare recordings. Just four LPs confirmed. STYLE: Standard mood music melodies and rhythms. MUSICIANS OF NOTE: Voices In Latin. SLEEVES: The same typographic design with simple changes in colour.

POUND

Nostalgia
Arawak
Solo piano moods. (JT)

HISTORY: Odd label from Rome, late 1970s. OUTPUT: Four LPs traced to date, probably at least ten in the catalogue. STYLE: Modern, jazzy, progressive, funky. MUSICIANS OF NOTE: Arawak. SLEEVES: Some strange period graphics and fonts.

PRIMA

Oriente Oggi
Rino De Filippi
East meets the hip West. (S)

HISTORY: Small Italian pop label. OUTPUT: One library LP produced. Rare to find. STYLE: Brilliant modern exotics. MUSICIANS OF NOTE: Rino De Filippi. SLEEVES: Appropriate illustration and font, but many issued in plain white sleeves.

PROGRAMME MUSIC

Shades of Rock
Projection. Includes guitarist
Rod Price from Fog Hat. (JD)

Hey Disco!
Trevor Basto
Post disco / electro sounds. (JT)

HISTORY: Established in London in 1971 by Joseph Weinberger to supply the BBC's Coded Music service. See also BMP (Audio), Impress, Joseph Weinberger, Tele Music. OUTPUT: Twenty-six LPs, all eventually incorporated into the Joseph Weinberger library catalogue. STYLE: Easy, jazz and rock, fine contemporary sounds. MUSICIANS OF NOTE: David Snell. SLEEVES: Generic purple with white type. However, the last sleeve in the series is black and not purple.

Minotaure Illustration 2
Christian Piget
Electronic and easy. (JT)

Ionic Scrabble
Claude Vasori
Experimental cues, repetitive rhythms. (SS)

HISTORY: A French label, based in Boulogne, early through to late 1970s. An offshoot of Musique Pour l'Image. OUTPUT: Approximately twenty releases covering a wide range of themes and ideas, rare and very desirable. Some sublicensing to Sylvester, with further international distribution via Brull. STYLE: Very conceptual releases, from African rhythms to deep soul, big band jazz and experimental electronics. MUSICIANS OF NOTE: Nancy Holloway, Manu Dibango, Martial Solal. SLEEVES: Graphics, collage, photography. No definitive house style.

Dinha Mantha's Power
Nancy Holloway (vocals)
Jazz, percussion, soul. (JT)

Locomotion
Martial Solal
Jazz forms. (C)

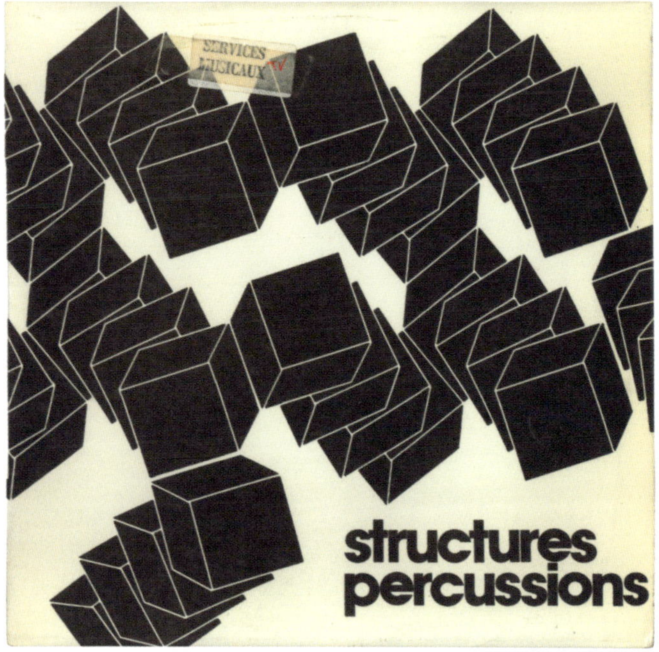

Structures Percussions
Charles Bellonzi and Robert Vigier
Abstract percussion. (JH)

The Hound Of Music
Georges Arvanitas Quartet
Modal jazz numbers. (JG)

African Voodoo
Manu Dibango
Rare African themes. (JG)

Chronoradial
Patrice Sciortino
Avant-garde percussion. (JH)

QUADRIGA

Q1
Heinz Kiessling and Peter Jaques, Orchestra Heuve
Jazz themes. (JG)

HISTORY: German label, dating from the early 1970s. Little traceable history. No sleevenotes or dates available. OUTPUT: Just three releases, Q1 to Q3. STYLE: Big band orchestral jazz. MUSICIANS OF NOTE: Heinz Kiessling. SLEEVES: Large 'Q' with number and colour changes.

RADIO RECORDS

Canta E Balla Le Tue Corse D'Estate
Various
Light, easy, groovy. (JT)

HISTORY: Mid-1960s Italian label started by Gian Piero Reverberi. OUTPUT: Seems to have started with library music, diversifying in the 1970s into commercial pop. Scarce and confusing output. Around forty LPs, but rarely seen. STYLE: From traditional jazz to progressive rock and electronic experiments. MUSICIANS OF NOTE: The Reverberi Group, Iron Stars (I Marc 4), The Underground Set. SLEEVES: Early editions have coloured sleeves with font and small chequered graphic devices. Later issues have standard disco sleeves with green and white chequered front and plain white backs, with or without tracklistings pasted on. Later issues have graphic or photographic sleeves.

Situazioni
Antonino Riccardo Luciani
Modern dramatics. (JP)

Fluid Trasparency
Franco Petrillo
Experimental. (JT)

HISTORY: Giant commercial recording company with several non-commercial international library labels. See also Fama, Fono Film, Iller, Jubal, New Tape, Pegaso, Ritmi E Canzoni, as well as April Orchestra Presents RCA Sound. OUTPUT: Library series as follows: RCA Custom 'Serie Mercurio' (over thirty LPs), SP Series (over a hundred releases including soundtracks), RCA Media LPs (numbered 1 to 27), RCA Koka Media LPs (numbered 28 to 60+), Dimensioni Sonore Series (ten LPs). Also sublicensing with CBS. STYLE: Every kind of music has been released across the various catalogues. MUSICIANS OF NOTE: Bruno Nicolai, Ennio Morricone, Romolo Grano, Nino Rota. SLEEVES: A wide variety of sleeves were produced across the different RCA ranges. Photography, collages, illustration, hard graphics and typography. Most series (and sub-series) have their own distinct style.

Esterni 1
Ennio Morricone, Giovanni Fusco etc
Pastoral / Western sound. (JT)

Romantici 2
Piero Piccione, Riz Ortolani, Bruno Nicolai etc
Musically, we are in love. (JT)

Musiche Leggere E Gaie 2
Ennio Morricone, Robby Poitevin, Piero Piccione etc
Easy and jazz cues. Classic SP Series. (JS)

Dimensioni Sonore 6
Bruno Nicolai
Spooky jazz and effects. Rare SP Series sleeve. (BH)

Dossier Special
Marco Melchiori
Synthesised ideas. (JP)

Cronache Dal Mondo
Lamartine
Progressive, experimental sounds. (JT)

Style
Gianni Oddi
Fine jazz and instrumentals. (JT)

Gimmick
Gianni Marchetti
Light orchestrals. (JT)

Daybreak
Group Meeting
Amazing light orchestrals and jazz. (JS)

Batterie
François Auger
Drum patterns and cues. RCA Media Series sleeve. (JD)

Robot Rose
Roland Bocquet
Cosmic claviers. (JP)

La Guerre Des Animaux
Philippe Besombes
Weird electronic ideas. (JT)

RCA Custom Series Volume 5
Gisteri, Romolo Grano
Space, murder, black leather gloves. (JT)

Action
Various artists
Dramatic odd sounds and compositions. (JT)

Tempo Jazz RCA Custom Series
Piero Umiliani
Classic early 1960s jazz session. (S)

READY MUSIC

Moog
Val Podlasinski
Moog spots and themes. (JT)

Moog II
Val Podlasinski
Further moogy dabbles. (JT)

HISTORY: Small London label, based in Covent Garden. Started in 1979. OUTPUT: At least twelve LPs produced throughout the 1980s. STYLE: Some short stings, dramatics, classic industrials and even some moogy action. MUSICIANS OF NOTE: John Leach, Trevor Jones, Peter Willshire. SLEEVES: All have the military band photo, with simple changes in colour and title.

RECORD TV DISCOGRAFICA (RTV)

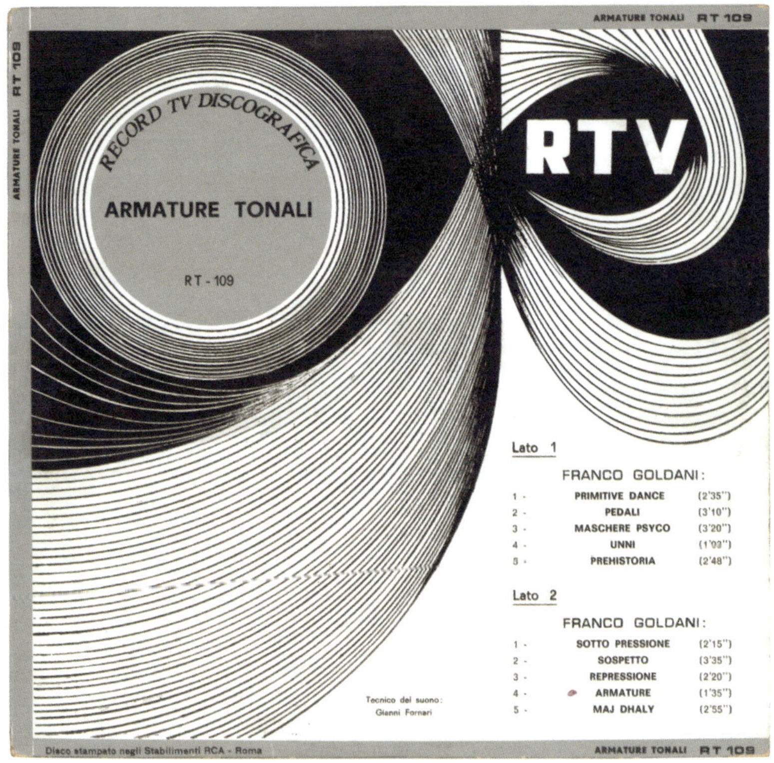

Armature Tonali
Franco Goldani
Drama and suspense cues. (JH)

HISTORY: Small Rome based label. See also Firmamento. OUTPUT: Possibly just eleven releases. Confusing range of catalogue numbers. STYLE: Electronics, jazz, conceptual. MUSICIANS OF NOTE: Sandro Brugnolini, Franco Goldani. SLEEVES: Generic graphic style with colour changes, one known LP has illustrations.

RED BUS

Themes For A One Man Band Volume 1
Alexander Goldsheider
Some progressive and sparse sounds. (JT)

HISTORY: UK label stared in 1983. OUTPUT: Eleven LPs issued over a four year period. STYLE: Experimental and sparse electronics, standard mood music cues. MUSICIANS OF NOTE: Alexander Goldsheider, John Fiddy. SLEEVES: All have the diagonal pinstripe with appropriate small image on the left.

REDIFFUSION

Mod: Rhythmic: Pop
Alan Moorhouse, The Disco Ten
Big band badness. (SG)

HISTORY: This library offshoot was started in 1971 by the British budget label Rediffusion in association with Carlton, a recording company based in New York. OUTPUT: Approximately sixteen LPs were made up until 1978. Most vinyl have yellow Carlton labels. STYLE: Easy listening, jazz, light orchestrals, some exotics and reggae pastiches. MUSICIANS OF NOTE: Sam Sklair, Alan Moorhouse, Ernest Berk. SLEEVES: A full colour Rediffusion International patterned sleeve, the same for every release. Titles and information only on the reverse.

REGENCY LINE

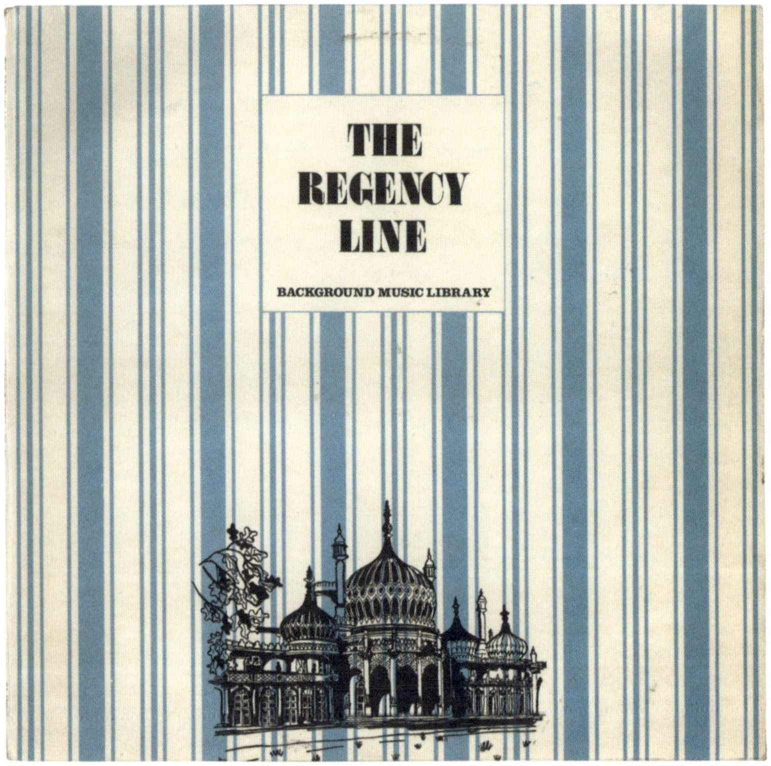

The Regency Line
Various moods and artists
A rare early sampler. (JG)

HISTORY: Small label from the UK, based in Brighton, c.1970. OUTPUT: Catalogue numbering suggests thirty-six LPs have been pressed, but many are hard to trace. STYLE: Jazz, pop, rock, dramatics, some electronics. MUSICIANS OF NOTE: Chris Rae. SLEEVES: Generic striped bag with an illustration of the Brighton Pavilion. Simple colour changes.

RHOMBUS

Biologia Marina
Includes Alessandroni, Giovanni Tommaso
Underwater experimental cues. (JD)

HISTORY: Italian label, started late 1970s. OUTPUT: Only one library LP found. Rare. See also Cenacolo, Nereide (as well as Cardium, Chic, Musical, Spring and Weekend), possibly all started by publisher Maria Stecchetti. STYLE: Minimal, electronic, avant-garde. MUSICIANS OF NOTE: Alessandro Alessandroni, Giovanni Tommaso. SLEEVES: Simple typography. High quality vinyl and thick card sleeves.

RING

Alchemy in Jazz
Oscar Rocchi
Various quintet recordings. (JT)

HISTORY: Rare Italian label, another subsidiary of Edizioni Musicali Minstrel in Rome. Linked to Flam, Fonovideo, Hard and World. OUTPUT: Small catalogue of nineteen with a few LPs put out for synchronisation. STYLE: Jazz, experimental, pastoral. MUSICIANS OF NOTE: Oscar Rocchi, Fabio Fabor. SLEEVES: No distinctive house style, paint splashes, typography, photography.

RITMI E CANZONI

The Keyboards 1
Enrico Riccardi
Piano experiments. (JT)

N.14 **Musicorama**
Enrico Riccardi, Ferdinando Onesti
Lively jazz, soul, fun. (S)

HISTORY: Early 1970s Italian label, part of the RCA library sprawl, see also Fama, Iller, Jubal and Pegaso. OUTPUT: Very small indeed. Noted mainly for the sought after Musicorama LP and one LP by Massimo Guantini. Rare LPs. STYLE: Jazz, rocky, groovy, some sinister moments. MUSICIANS OF NOTE: Enrico Riccardi, Sandro Brugnolini. SLEEVES: Stock photo with typography, some LPs have just typography.

RKM MUSIC LIBRARY

Beat – Action
Sluszny, Dero, Lucas
Funky travel and movement. (JT)

HISTORY: Large rock, pop and classical Belgian label founded by music producer Roland Kluger. OUTPUT: Just three LPs made specifically for library usage. STYLE: Progressive jazz, lively Latin and funk. MUSICIANS OF NOTE: Nico Gomez (Joseph van het Groenewoud), John Sluszny and Ralph Benatar (El Chicles). SLEEVES: Green generic sleeve with logo and title.

ROBERT E. VIGIER
(REV)

The Pink Magic
Georges Arvanitas Trio
Slow and medium tempo jazz styles. (S)

HISTORY: French label started in 1976, ended in 1977. OUTPUT: Very small, just three LPs traced. STYLE: Euro jazz. MUSICIANS OF NOTE: Robert Vigier. SLEEVES: One colour designs using illustration.

ROBERT HALL

New World W-23 / 24
Anonymous artist
Percussion and rock. (JT)

HISTORY: Large stable of American production music, including SFX. We believe it started in New York in the 1960s. OUTPUT: Difficult to accurately assess production runs, catalogue numbers suggest hundreds across various Robert Hall productions, including the expansive New World series. STYLE: Jingles to dramatics, industrials and novelties. MUSICIANS OF NOTE: Keith Foley, John Danser and Bill Loose, but many albums credit no composer. SLEEVES: Plain disco bags, branded 'Robert Hall Production' disco bags in blue or yellow, some plain sleeves with pasted on tracklistings, some blank paper sleeves.

ROMAN RECORD COMPANY (RRC)

Spazio
Gianni Mazza
Rare spooky abstract sounds. (JS)

HISTORY: Active between 1968 and 1973, this Italian record company was founded by Gaetano Pulvirenti and Giovanni Fischietti. OUTPUT: Small run of very sought after LPs, especially those in the series *Viaggio Attraverso I Problemi Dell'Uomo* (a trip into the problems of man). STYLE: Jazzy, lively, progressive, psychedelic. MUSICIANS OF NOTE: Enzo Scoppa, Gianni Mazza. Silvano Chimenti. SLEEVES: Early library sleeves all have the checkered psychedelic design, with simple changes in titles. Later library sleeves have the TV illustration.

ROTARY

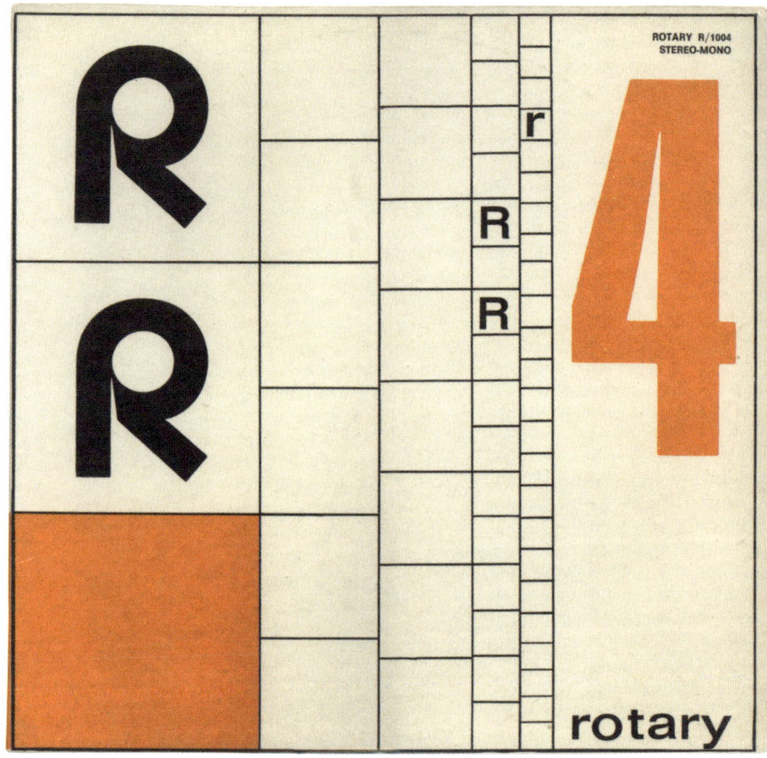

Situazioni E Sensazioni
Viostel
Super groovy sounds. (JS)

Jazz Video Rotary 4
Farlocco (aka Giuliano Sorgini)
Dark jazz moods. (JT)

HISTORY: Small Italian label started by composer and pianist Amedeo Tommasi. OUTPUT: Just seven releases between 1973 and 1974. STYLE: Jazz, easy, experimental. MUSICIANS OF NOTE: Mainly pseudonyms, Sandro Brugnolini, Stefano Torossi. SLEEVES: Grid style with changes in colour and number.

Cobra
H. Haseley and E. Marving
Wide variety of melodic group numbers. (JM)

Red Kite
Astral Sounds
Electronic music for water and nature. (JD)

HISTORY: Founded in 1973, a subsidiary of the giant De Wolfe library. OUTPUT: Over eighty LPs. STYLE: Rock to electronics and beyond. SLEEVES: Graphics and illustration. Distinctive De Wolfe style.

Superdoop
Simon Park
Electronic music by Chameleon. (MG)

Glass Head
F. McDonald and C. Rae
Very modern group sounds, funky rock. (LV)

Hard As Rock
J. Bunny-Browne
Guitar based rock played by Knockout. (MG)

Blackout
A. Valotti
Dramatic group pieces. Sleeve design by Logo Ltd. (JM)

RYTHM AND BLUES

The Heaven Blues
More light jazz. (JG)

Georgio and The Heaven Blues
Light jazz. (JG)

HISTORY: Mid-1960s Paris based label. OUTPUT: Small number of pressings, only a handful of releases. Produced and distributed via SIMM. Now rare. STYLE: Fairly straight mood themes, some jazz. SLEEVES: Graphics and paintings. No LP titles, instead they are all named after the groups who recorded the music.

SABLE

Andros
Mixer
Odd futuristic sounds. (JD)

HISTORY: An obscure Italian label, late 1970s. OUTPUT: Five LPs traced. STYLE: Fairly standard library cues, also some contemporary electronics. MUSICIANS OF NOTE: Pseudonyms mostly used. SLEEVES: Bizarre fonts, collage and art.

117 **Futurissimo**
Egisto Macchi
Experimental electronic sounds. (JD)

HISTORY: A continuation of MP2000, set up for Italian library licensing. OUTPUT: Average size label, made up of unique and sublicensed Italian recordings. Twenty-three releases traced, some from Omicron, Liuto, Gemelli, Deneb. STYLE: Italian style, from easy to experimental, some fine percussion. MUSICIANS OF NOTE: Egisto Macchi, Alessandro Alessandroni, Piero Umiliani. SLEEVES: Strong graphic style. Some illustration.

108 **OPUS 3 14 16**
A. Sáinz and L. Sáinz
Progressive sounds. (JG)

102 **Les Vocalises Modernes**
A. Alessandroni
Vocal jazz and improvised chorals. (JT)

107 **Symbolisme Psychedelique**
G. Iacoucci
Weird atmospheres, space. (JH)

SELECTED SOUND

Montage 9000 Series
Gerhard Trede
German musical experiments. (JD)

Funky Eyes ST Series
Zbig Górny
Modern love from 1982. (JT)

HISTORY: Large quality German label set up in 1968 by Klaus Netzle. OUTPUT: Expansive catalogue of fine pressings. The 9000 Series runs to over a hundred and twenty LPs, with the ST Series (started in 1973) running to over ninety LPs. STYLE: Proggy, rocky and percussive, conceptual library recordings, some jazz and easy. MUSICIANS OF NOTE: Roland Kovac, Klaus Weiss. SLEEVES: Large family of distinctive gold sleeves for the first series, period illustration, photography and graphic crimes for the ST catalogue. FAMOUS CUES: Some BBC Schools interval music. Some pornography.

SELECTION RECORDS

My Lovely Planet
Jacques Siroul
Computer music. (JT)

HISTORY: Belgian music library company, operating from the mid-1970s onwards. OUTPUT: Two series of library albums pressed, running to a total of nineteen LPs. STYLE: Modern industrials, light classical, easy, jazz, experimental. MUSICIANS OF NOTE: Janko Nilovic, René Costy, Dan Lacksman. SLEEVES: One series has dynamic op art sleeves, the other a less exciting illustration in two colours.

SEVEN MEN

Da'Il Cinghialetto
Gianni Ferrio
Jazz, experiments. (S)

HISTORY: Tiny Italian label, operating in the early 1970s. OUTPUT: Just two LPs found. STYLE: Jazz industrials. MUSICIANS OF NOTE: Gianni Ferrio. SLEEVES: Simple bold numbers printed in one colour.

01. **Sunrise Sunset / Strange And Mysterious**
Souc / Denjean
Cosmic, peculiar. (JT)

02. **Rhythm Section**
Hauser / Rioland
More cosmic and peculiar music. (S)

HISTORY: Independent French label started in Paris by composer Pierre Roussat. OUTPUT: Very small. Possibly only two LPs made. No release dates available, late 1970s. STYLE: Experimental, groovy, progressive. MUSICIANS OF NOTE: José Souc, Jacques Denjean. SLEEVES: Simple but appropriate glossy silver and gold sleeve with diagonal coloured band.

SOEDI

Serie Gialli
Lester Freeman (Enrico Intra)
Evil giallo sounds. (JT)

HISTORY: Early 1980s Italian pop label. OUTPUT: A handful of rare and bizarre releases for use in TV. STYLE: Jazz based giallo scores. MUSICIANS OF NOTE: Pino Calvi, Lester Freeman. SLEEVES: Simple graphics, some confusing elements, such as two labels on one LP and unusual catalogue numbers.

Black Sun
Various artists
Tangos and oriental themes.
Photograph by Yves Van Waerbeke. (S)

The Boss Music Volume 1. Kitten Kind
Jean-Claude Pierric
Jazz. (S)

HISTORY: Obscure Paris based label, c.1972. OUTPUT: Very few relases, thirteen LPs traced. STYLE: Experimental, atmospheric, jazzy, electronic. MUSICIANS OF NOTE: Gérard Doulssane, Jean-Claude Pierric. SLEEVES: An unpredictable blend of images and type.

Sprint In Fashion
Mainardi / Romano
Light trendy numbers. (SG)

Funky Rock's Selection
Bakesky Group
No rock, no funk. (JT)

HISTORY: Bizarre Italian label, possibly from the late 1970s. OUTPUT: Only these two LPs traced. STYLE: Unpredictable. SLEEVES: Questionable typography.

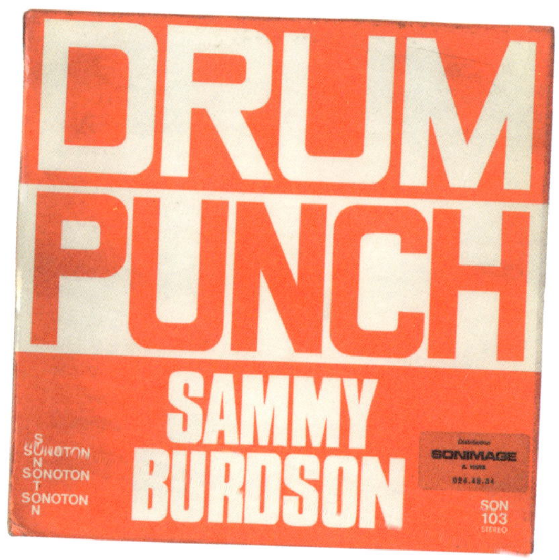

SON101 **Amazing Space** Volume 1
Mladen Franko
Experimental themes. (JD)

SON122 **Swinging Centuries** Volume 1
Various artists
Updated period music. (JD)

SON113 **Under Water** Volume 1
Walt Rockman
Submersed sounds. Multi Sound Music sticker. (JD)

SON103 **Drum Punch**
Sammy Burdson
Percussive cues. (JD)

SON105 **Contemporary Sounds and Movements**
Volume 2
Mladen Franko
New sounds for current affairs. (JM)

SON168 **The Micro Chip Revolution**
Sam Sklair and Gus Galbraith
Electronics. (JM)

SOUNDS OF BROADCASTING

SON178 **Sport Sequences** Volume 2
Klaus Weiss
Light / heavy activity. (JD)

Standard SOB sleeve.
No artists' credits. (LV)

HISTORY: Part of the William B. Tanner Company. Memphis based, possibly mid-1970s. OUTPUT: Large and varied. STYLE: Vast range of classical and electronic background styles. MUSICIANS OF NOTE: No musicians ever credited. SLEEVES: Generic golden house style.

SOUND STAGE

The New World
Ann Dudley
New equipment, new music. (JT)

HISTORY: Offshoot of the Amphonic label, started in 1981. OUTPUT: Large catalogue of at least fifty albums. STYLE: Jingles, jazz, percussion, underlays and experimental electronics MUSICIANS OF NOTE: Ann Dudley, Frank Ricotti, David Snell. SLEEVES: Early albums have distinctive red sleeves with black and white typography, later with simple graphics, then drab stock photography or full 'art sleeves'.

SOUND WORK SHOP

Discomusic
Rovi (Piero Umiliani)
Oddly, not disco music. (JT)

HISTORY: Independent Italian label, started in Rome by composer and artist Piero Umiliani in 1967. See also Liuto, Omicron, Telesound and Videovoice (and Ciak). OUTPUT: At least twenty-two LPs traced. Original jazz sessions; rare soundtrack scores also pressed for background usage. Some distribution via MP2000. Highly sought after. STYLE: Varied in style and quality, some improvisation and electronics mixed with folk. MUSICIANS OF NOTE: Alessandro Alessandroni, Piero Umiliani. Pseudonyms also used. SLEEVES: House style on the reverse only. Collage and graphics dominate. Inconsistent catalogue numbers.

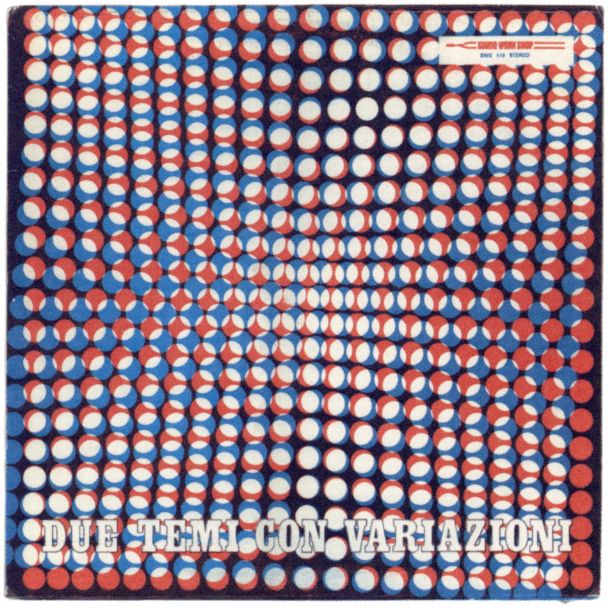

La Ragazza Fuoristrada
Piero Umiliani
Full score as background music. (S)

Due Temi Con Variazioni
Rovi
Jazz improvisations. (I)

L'Uomo E La Città
Piero Umiliani
Also a Liuto release. (S)

News!!! News!!!
Moggi (Piero Umiliani)
Jazz and documentary style cues. (I)

Il Corpo
Piero Umiliani
Legendary soundtrack issued as library.
Multi Sound Music sticker. (JP)

Olimpiade SWS111
Santucci Scoppa
Rare sporting themes, jazz instrumentation.
MP2000 distribution sticker. (JG)

The Folk Group
Zalla
Rock sounds, includes *Underworld*. (JT)

SOUTHERN

7" MQ series
Westway Studio Orchestra

Standard Southern UK sleeve. (JT)

HISTORY: London label based in Denmark Street, mid-1960s onwards. Run by Dennis Berry (aka Peter Dennis) who also started the contemporary mood music label known as Peer International. OUTPUT: Well over two hundred releases across 7", 10" and LP. Large international distribution network. Licensed recordings from international artists as well as original sessions. Some rare 7" issues, with non-LP tracks. 9000 Series are represses of Peer International LPs. STYLE: European easy, jazz, classical, percussion and electronics. MUSICIANS OF NOTE: Nino Nardini, Johnny Scott, Bernard Ebbinghouse. SLEEVES: 7" records have plain white bag. LPs have generic blue and white sleeves.

SPIDER

One Guitar and Many Guitars
Bruno Battisti D'Amario
Daring compositions. Re-badged Vedette sleeve. (JT)

HISTORY: Italian label, from 1970. Sub-label of Vedette. OUTPUT: Very small, only three LPs traced, all with Vedette 'VSM' catalogue numbers. STYLE: Progressive sounds, pop electronics, western style guitar. MUSICIANS OF NOTE: The Distortions / Blue Phantom, Armando Sciascia. SLEEVES: Two LPs with different Vedette sleeves, one with unique artwork.

SQUIRREL

Psyco Analysis
Corviria
Electronics and pastoral sounds. (JT)

Accadde A.......
Arawak
Experimental cues. (SS)

HISTORY: Small independent Italian label, c.1972. OUTPUT: Five LPs found, but catalogue numbering runs to at least seventeen (possibly dreamt up by an actual squirrel). STYLE: Experimental, dramatic. MUSICIANS OF NOTE: All artists used pseudonyms. SLEEVES: Mixture of styles using graphics and painting.

SR
(SERMI)

Intermezzi No.4. SR Jazz Series
Alessandro Alessandroni
Folded sleeve. Includes *Yazz In Calcutta* (sic). (JT)

HISTORY: 1960s Italian label developed out of the Sermi Cable production company. OUTPUT: Prolific but obscure releases, mainly Italian only distribution. Random sublicensing to the UK (Conroy) and France (St Germain Des Prés). Some vanity pressings. Approximately forty LPs. Now rare. STYLE: Broad and varied, classical, baroque, experimental, jazz and psychedelia. MUSICIANS OF NOTE: Alessandro Alessandroni, Armando Trovajoli, I Marc 4, Giovanni Tommaso. SLEEVES: Some issued in plain sleeves with Sermi Film stamp and catalogue numbers scribbled on the front. Some have hard card sleeves, others flimsy and often unglued paper. Varied art, graphic or photographic sleeves.

Alessandro Alessandroni
Alessandro Alessandroni
Psychedelic jazz and progressive easy. (S)

Alessandro Alessandroni E Il Suo Complesso
Alessandro Alessandroni
Very beautiful music. (S)

Nel Mondo Del Lavoro
Rino De Filippi
Fine, metronomic industrials. (MK)

In Modo Serioso
Franco Tamponi
Classical and avant compositions. (JT)

Dimensione Umana
Alessandro Alessandroni
Includes *Laugh In Beat.* (JT)

Music Ed Elettronica
Gino Marinuzzi Jr.
Wild electronics. (MK)

SP Series
Armando Trovajoli and I Marc 4
Italian mood music meets swinging London. (JT)

Shopping In Carnaby Street
Various
Jazz for consumption. (JT)

Indefinitive Atmosphere SP Series
Giovanni Tommaso
Bass driven jazz and avant jazz. (JT)

Rhythms In Suspense SP Series
Gino Marinuzzi Jr.
Dark sonic moods. (JT)

Open Air Parade ST Series
Alessandro Alessandroni
Psychedelic jazz and psychedelic easy. (JT)

Rebus ST Series
Alessandro Alessandroni
Experimental oddities and atmospheres. (JT)

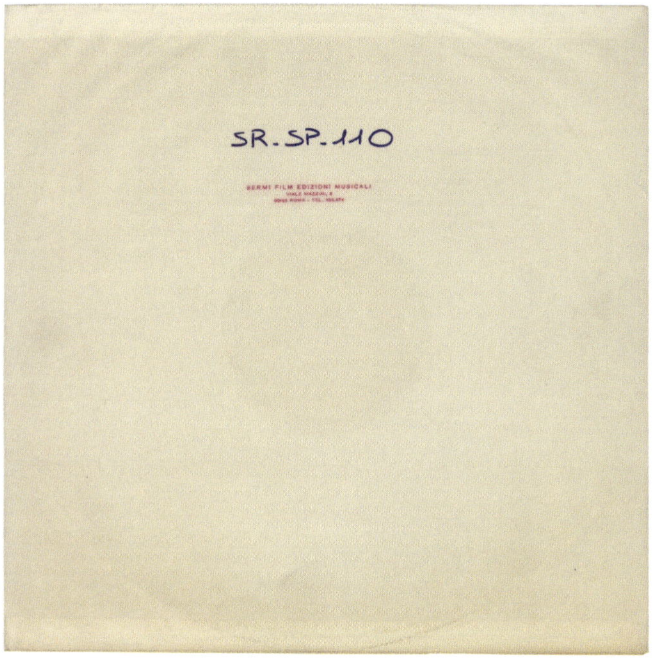

SR SP 110 Issued in plain, stamped sleeve
Alessandroni E Il Suo Complesso
Improvised easy listening. (JT)

Vacanze
Rino De Filippi
Fine holiday rhythms and sounds. (JK)

Miscellanea
Zito
Unusual and interesting sounds. (JT)

Atmosfera Bellica
Alessandro Alessandroni
Music of war (S)

STANDARD

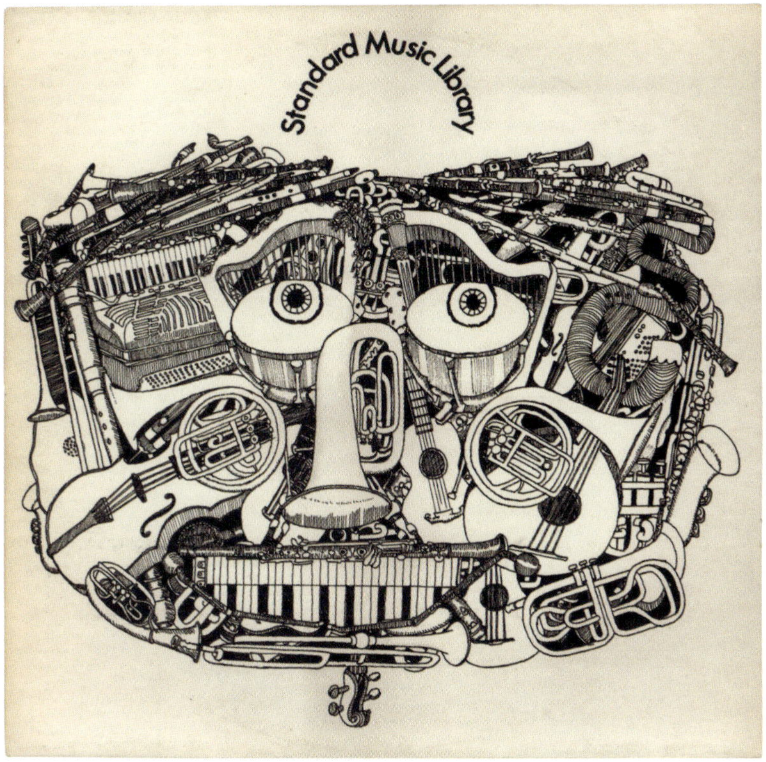

Early single colour 'face' sleeve. (JT)

ESL 168 (withdrawn)
Brian Eno
Textures. (JT)

HISTORY: Vast independent London label, founded in 1968. Set up by Essex Music Group and LWT, this was the first music publishing company to be owned jointly with a broadcaster. OUTPUT: Large and regular pressings throughout the 1960s and 1970s. STYLE: All styles produced, from big band to electronic experimentation. MUSICIANS OF NOTE: Brian Eno, David Vorhaus, Herbie Flowers, Delia Derbyshire, Ron Grainer, Sam Fonteyn. SLEEVES: Single colour face made up of musical instruments, changing to film strip colour sleeve in the late 1970s. The withdrawn Brian Eno LP has a unique logo design. FAMOUS CUES: *Catweasel*, *On The Buses*, *Please Sir*, *Budgie*, *Crimestoppers*.

STUDIO 7

Brivididi

HISTORY: Interesting Italian label started c.1969. OUTPUT: A few LPs, some made for synchronisation, then repressed as commercial LPs. STYLE: Light, easy, hip. MUSICIANS OF NOTE: Elvio Monti. SLEEVES: Pretty groovy.

STUDIO G

Images
P. Willsher and T. Kelly
Disco, and modern rhythms. (JM)

HISTORY: Medium sized but far reaching British label, established c.1970 by John Gale, hence the 'G' in Studio G. See also Parry. OUTPUT: Forty-eight LPs and a series of earlier library singles. Some quite hard to find and desirable. STYLE: Rock, jazz, horror, humour, electronics. SLEEVES: Period graphics, normally two colour process printing. All sleeves have theme logos in the bottom right corner. Most artwork by Nina Klein. FAMOUS CUES: *The Chesty Morgan* theme, *Drag Racer* used for BBC Snooker, *Vision-On* incidentals.

Beat Group
Mike Lease (arranger and organist)
Progressive cues. (S)

Cool Beat
Robert Cornford
Heavy dance numbers. (JG)

Avant Garde
D. Detoni, John Keliehor, John Lewis
Abstract electronics and ethereal processed vocals. (C)

Dramatic and Horror
Paul Lewis, David De Lara, Robert Cornford, James Harpham, Stan Medcalf
Tension, suspense, shock. (JM)

Descriptive Suites
Paul Lewis and James Harpham (SS)

Electronic Age
Electronics, concrete, voodoo.
Artwork by Nina Klein. (SS)

Drama and Horror
Paul Lewis
Dark movements in jazz. (JT)

Music For Synthesizers
Eric Peters
Subtle electronic beds and abstractions. (JT)

Industrial Underscore
Douglas Wood
Space folk music. (JT)

Racing Tempo
Eric Towren
Fast, swinging jazz themes. 10" release. (S)

Zenith
Eric Towren
Space and underwater sounds, percussion based. (JT)

Voices In The Wind
The Paris Studio Group
Jazz and scat themes. 10" release. (MG)

HISTORY: London based, originally songsheet publishers, part of the De Wolfe empire. Moved into 33rpm library records in the mid-1960s. See also De Wolfe, PSI. OUTPUT: Over fifty LPs and 10" albums. Some sub-publishing with Musique Pour l'Image. SLEEVES: Early stunning graphics, later generic white and gold circle design.

City In Terror / Sextopraxis
W. Warren
Rare concept LP. Front and back cover. (S)

Sysmo Volume 1
Bonnet, Romanelli
Cosmic carnage. Two LP set. (JT)

HISTORY: Experimental 1980s French label, based in Paris, associated with Hibou. OUTPUT: From 1982 onwards the label issued at least eight LPs, including some double albums. STYLE: Interesting electronics, jingles, abstract music made using the Sculptures Sonores, some avant-garde compositions, some world music. MUSICIANS OF NOTE: Roland Romanelli, Sergio Otanazetra. SLEEVES: Photography, graphics, illustration, some with matching boxed based sleeves. The 'shatter' logo is both prominent and consistent.

Rare Impress 'Audio' sublicensed 10" disc
Syd Dale
Includes *Marching There And Back*.

Vibrations
Bernard Lubat
Jazz, beats. (JT)

HISTORY: Important Paris label, founded by producer Roger Tokarz in 1968. OUTPUT: Massive international output. Over one hundred releases on 10" and 12". Some sublicensing. Consistently high quality recordings. Unusual and early collaboration with Impress ('Audio') library also found. STYLE: Electronics, percussion, experimentals, jazz and funky rhythms. MUSICIANS OF NOTE: Bernard Lubat, Guy Pedersen, Bernard Estardy, Raymond Guiot. SLEEVES: Standard house style, with simple colour and logo variations. Later used graphics and stock photography.

Spatial & Co
Sauveur Mallia
Late European 'disco' sound. (JM)

Suspence Elettronica
Tusco
Ambient electronic meanderings. (JT)

HISTORY: Tiny Italian label from 1983, another Piero Umiliani offshoot. See also Liuto, Omicron, Sound Work Shop, Videovoice (and Ciak). OUTPUT: Only three LPs traced. STYLE: Pastoral, experimental, electronic. MUSICIANS OF NOTE: All music by Umiliani under the name of either Tusco or Catamo. SLEEVES: Pictorial sleeves with simple graphics and colour.

Mystery Movie
James Clarke
Driving and funky underscores. (S)

New Blood
Alan Parker and Alan Hawkshaw
Heavy rhythmic pop. (S)

HISTORY: London based library label, founded by musician Alan Parker in the mid-1970s. OUTPUT: Over fifty LPs developed throughout the late 1970s. Now owned by EMI. Most sessions recorded in Germany. STYLE: Rock, funk, comedy, romance. MUSICIANS OF NOTE: Alan Parker, Alan Hawkshaw. SLEEVES: Mustard colour background with illustrations in various styles. FAMOUS CUES: Drama Suites 1 & 2 used in *The Hanged Man* produced by Yorkshire TV, *Grange Hill* theme, *Winner Takes All*.

Breath of Danger
Hawkshaw and Bennett
Suspense and drama backcloths. (JM)

The All American Powerhouse
Alan Parker and Alan Hawkshaw
Guitar based funk. (S)

Timing No.1
Stéphane Grappelli, Jacky Giordano
Insane beats. (JG)

Timing No.2
Yan Tregger, Roger Bourdin
Interesting moods. (JT)

Timing No.3
Tregger / Giordano / Devevy / Legrand
Cool vocal jazz. (JT)

Timing No.4
Roger Bourdin, Jacky Giordano
More hip sounds. (JT)

Timing No.5
Jacky Nodaro, Stéphane Grappelli
Light folk / jazz. (JT)

Timing No.6
Giordano / Jerome / Kaufman
Experimental fusions. (JT)

HISTORY: Label started as part of In Editions, Paris, early 1970s. OUTPUT: Just sixteen LPs pressed. Early issues are hard to find and very desirable. From Timing No.7 onwards the label is split with De Wolfe as Timing In Éditions. STYLE: Trad jazz to electronics. MUSICIANS OF NOTE: Jacky Giordano, Stéphane Grappelli, Pierre Avary. SLEEVES: Simple two colour graphic sleeves for the first six releases, changing over the next ten using different fonts, some illustration and photography, with unusual dotted spines.

nº 3
timing

nº 4
timing

nº 5
timing

nº 6
timing

TITIAN

Descriptive
Corviria
Synthesised themes.
Includes *Evil's Suite*. (JD)

HISTORY: Late 1970s Italian independent label, Milan based. OUTPUT: Just a few LPs traced, but catalogue numbers suggest up to seventeen LPs may have been made. STYLE: Filmic, quite odd. MUSICIANS OF NOTE: Luciano Simoncini (Arawak). SLEEVES: Simple, graphic.

TRANSWORLD RECORDED LIBRARY

TR 77, 78 RPM
Johnny Dankworth
Miserable jazz drama. (JP)

HISTORY: Early 1950s library label based in Denmark Street, London. OUTPUT: At least one hundred releases, all on 78rpm. Few have survived. STYLE: Short exotic cues. MUSICIANS OF NOTE: Bernard Herrmann, Pierre Henry, Jerry Goldsmith (as Jerrald Goldsmith). SLEEVES: As with all 78rpm library records we have found, there are no printed sleeves, just cardboard record 'bags' taped on three sides.

TVMUSIC

Crazy Sounds / Weird Sounds
Cecil Leuter
Electronics. TVM house bag. (SS)

HISTORY: Part of the giant Chappell organisation, c.1973. OUTPUT: Just four LPs issued. An Italian version of the label issued at least two different LPs with an IT catalogue prefix. STYLE: Experimental, electronics, percussion. MUSICIANS OF NOTE: Cecil Leuter. SLEEVES: Blue and white with TVMusic logo. TVM 103 and 104 have the catalogue number on the disco bag. Italian LPs have the same sleeve design but in black and white.

TWO NUNS

Musiche Di Ugalberto De Angelis
Ugalberto De Angelis
Classcial cues and contemporary ideas. (S)

HISTORY: Commercial label started by the Two Nuns publishing company, Italy. OUTPUT: A couple of library based LPs across a small catalogue of film music and easy listening, c.1972. STYLE: Classical, avant-garde. MUSICIANS OF NOTE: Pietro Grossi, Ugalberto De Angelis. SLEEVES: A mixture of graphics and typography.

UBM RECORDS

(UWE BUSCHKÖTTER MUSIC)

Computer Energy UBM Volume 8
Various artists
Guitars, arp, moog, prophet work. (LV)

HISTORY: Cologne based label. Founded c.1980 by Uwe Buschkötter, a long-standing arranger of jazz and easy music. OUTPUT: Approximately twenty LPs made for library use. STYLE: Anything from jazz to jingles. MUSICIANS OF NOTE: The Earforce Band. SLEEVES: Simple, using a black and white graphic house style.

UNI DISC

Metamorphoses
F. Semprun and M. Christodoulides
More music for dance expression. (JH)

HISTORY: Medium sized Paris based label dating from the early 1960s. Now owned by Auvidis. OUTPUT: Large catalogue of experimental, religious, ballet and children's recordings, many offered to TV stations for library music usage. STYLE: Experimental, industrial. MUSICIANS OF NOTE: André Huet, Sylvio Gualda. SLEEVES: Strong graphic and fantasy feel. Some photography on earlier issues.

UNITED ARTISTS

UAM 2
Leroy Holmes
Pop instrumentals. (SG)

Imaginations
André Huet
Music for dance expression. (JH)

Imaginations / 2
André Huet
Music for dance expression. (JH)

HISTORY: Experimental synchronisation catalogue for music industry giant. OUTPUT: Unusual catalogue of just two LPs, both pressed in the UK. These were instrumental LPs repressed for use as library music. STYLE: Pop, easy listening. MUSICIANS OF NOTE: Leroy Holmes, The Bobby Wilson Connection. SLEEVES: Inappropriate 1930s ballroom style design, which may explain the instant failure of the catalogue.

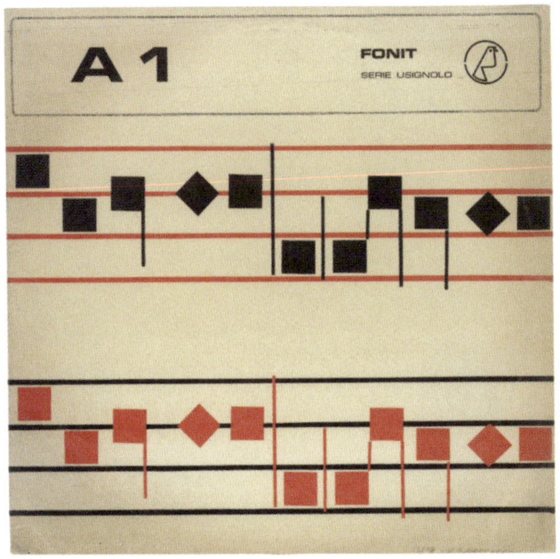

A1 **Antichi E Arcaici**
Enrico Colonese
Fine ancient sounds. (JT)

B172 **Ballabili Vari**
Enrico Colonese
Psychedelics, modal jazz. (S)

C267 **Caratteristici**
Giampiero Boneschi
Solo experimental electronics. (JT)

HISTORY: : This is the main label for most of Fonit / Fonit Cetra's library releases. See also Goldfinger. OUTPUT: Impressive and important catalogue of over one hundred LPs starting in 1970. The whole Fonit / Usignolo / Goldfinger catalogues are very confusing, with single or multiple company logos and unpredictable numbering systems. It appears that the Usignolo catalogues start at A1, B81, B171, C261, C361, D401, F501, GST337, H601, I651, P881 with a long sporadic series beginning with the UST prefix starting at UST4 (following on from A3). If you are still with us, there are also LPs that are simply titled with a group or a musical style, and some LPs have one company logo on the sleeve and a completely different one on the label. STYLE: Anything and everything from early music to progressive electronics. Some truly remarkable music. MUSICIANS OF NOTE: Boneschi, Mario Molino, I Marc 4, Giuliano Sorgini, Alessandro Alessandroni. Pino Calvi, Basso Valdambrini. SLEEVES: Many LPs across several series have the same artwork (spin painting, paint splashes, abstract art, collage, period photography etc) with simple changes in number on the top bar. Most have the nightingale logo. Also some unpredictable and unique sleeve designs.

UST 334 **Atmosfere E Sensazioni**
Cincinnato
Various fine musical moods. (S)

UST 370 **Caratteristici Vari**
Alessandro Alessandroni
Amazing guitar sounds. (MK)

UST 701 **Religiosi E Cerimoniali**
Censi, Valle
Vatican sounds. (S)

Postal Area Group
Gian Piero Reverberi, Chiplin
Two sides of good jazz. (S)

B84 **Ballabili Anni '70**
Fabio Fabor
Samba, bossa, protests. (JT)

UST 369 **Caratterstici Vari**
Carlo Esposito, Antonio Altamura
Jazz, gangsters, bossa nova. (S)

Soft Music 4
I Marc 4
Easy / jazz. (JT)

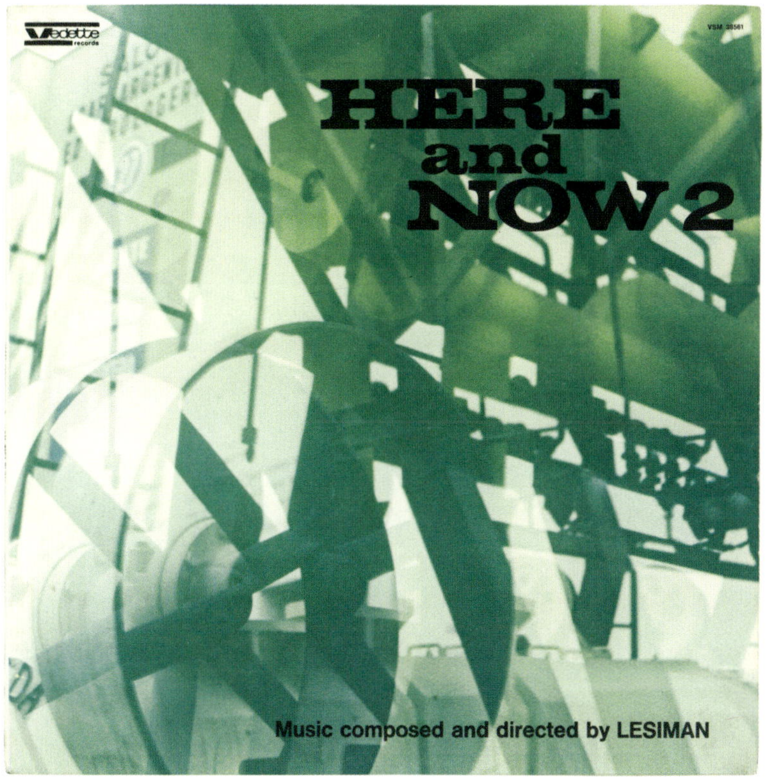

Here and Now 1
Lesiman
Intense rhythmic grooves, heavy on effects. (C)

Here and Now 2
Lesiman
A continuation of Here and Now 1. (SS)

HISTORY: Milan based label from the late 1960s onwards, started by film composer Armando Sciascia. See also Spider. OUTPUT: Very large set of releases for library and synchronisation across different series. Sublicensing to Ember. STYLE: Notable spaghetti style output, jazz. Also classic Italian style giallo horror themes. MUSICIANS OF NOTE: Bruno Battisti, Lesiman, Armando Sciascia. SLEEVES: Standard design using three swirls (see Spider), later employing photography and graphics for the different series.

Bittersweet Moods
H. Tical, Alex Brown
From stomps to snakes. (JT)

Violin Reactions
Armando Sciascia
Electronic violin with beats. (JT)

Sea Fantasy
Armando Sciascia
Amazing underwater concepts. (JT)

VIDEOVOICE

High Tension Volume 1
Lesiman
Modern, dark dramatics and underscores. (JT)

Double Face
Moggi
Five compositions played twice, electronic, classical. (JT)

HISTORY: Italian label run by Piero Umiliani. See also Liuto, Omicron, Sound Work Shop and Telesound (and Ciak). OUTPUT: Very small catalogue dating from 1981, just three LPs traced. Catalogue numbers are sequential with others on Umiliani's labels. STYLE: Dramatic, classical, progressive, electronic. MUSICIANS OF NOTE: All music by Piero Umiliani under his Moggi or Catamo pseudonyms. SLEEVES: Mixture of odd period graphics and fonts.

VI DI ELLE / EDIZIONI DISCOGRAFICHE VI DI ELLE / VDL (VOCE DEL LIRI)

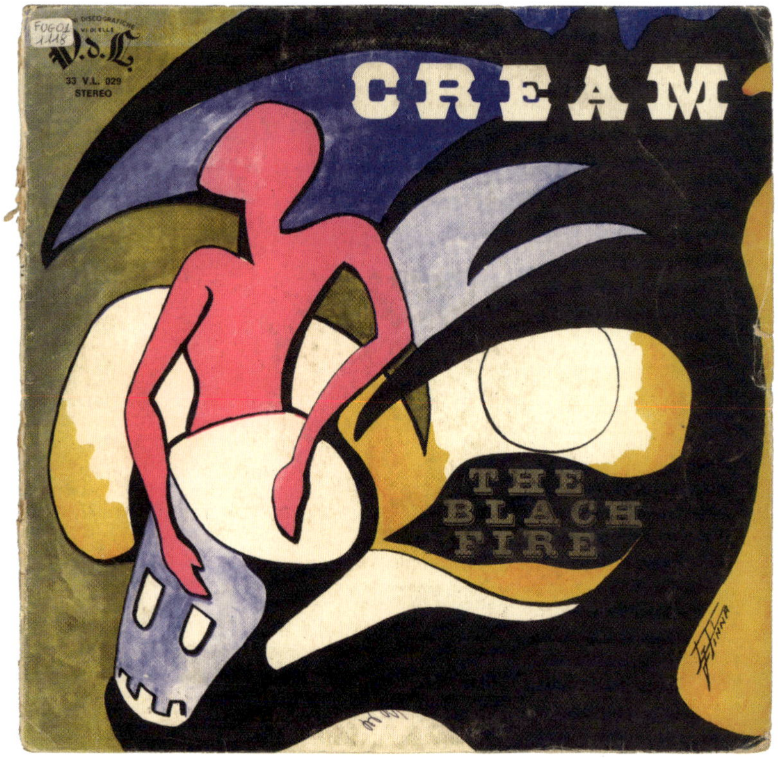

Cream
The Black Fire
Progressive sambas and bossa novas. (MK)

HISTORY: Bizarre label from the early 1970s. OUTPUT: Very few LPs traced. The confusing catalogue / label name cannot help. We have found one library based LP, that also appears on the Flirt label. STYLE: Pretty groovy. MUSICIANS OF NOTE: The Black Fire. SLEEVES: Some quite daring art, painted by G. Pinna.

VIVO MUSIC

Many Moods from Vivo
Edwin Astley
1980s Electronic Edwin (JT)

HISTORY: Label started in 1980 by TV composing legend Edwin Astley. Based in Moulsford-on-Thames. OUTPUT: Just two LPs traced, there maybe more based on catalogue numbers which start at seventeen. STYLE: Interesting library sounds and ideas made on a Fairlight, with some period accompaniment and production. MUSICIANS OF NOTE: Edwin Astley. SLEEVES: Simple two colour hand drawn type. LPs often come with a typed insert explaining that the LPs are library music.

Love
Mario Molino And His Group
Rare double library LP. (S)

Ambiente E Musica
Antonio Ricardo Luciani
Free electronics. (JP)

HISTORY: Late 1960s Italian label. OUTPUT: Fifteen LPs traced. Some licensing to Sonimage in France. Fairly poor distribution. One of the few libraries to issue double LPs. Now rare. STYLE: Alternative, rocky, a little jazz. MUSICIANS OF NOTE: Mario Molino. SLEEVES: No house style. Paintings, graphics, photography.

WILD CAT

La Palla é Rotonda
Remigio Ducros
Jazz and sporting themed concepts. (JG)

Giardino Dei Miei Desideri
Rino De Filippi
Sublime and classic De Filippi. (JS)

HISTORY: Strange and small Italian label with unpredictable releases. OUTPUT: Possibly as many as fifteen LPs from the late 1960s onwards. Rare. STYLE: Jazz, dramatics, easy listening, some conceptual recordings. MUSICIANS OF NOTE: Walter Rizzati, Giuliano Sorgini, Rino De Filippi. SLEEVES: No definitive house style – a mix of simple graphics, illustration, photography and fonts.

WILLIAM B. TANNER

The CAT (Creative Advertising Themes) Issue 34
No artists credited
Moog, rythms, fuzz, donuts. (JT)

HISTORY: Large American based library label and jingle house. Origins go back to the Pepper Sound Studios in 1957, the William B. Tanner group rising in 1972. OUTPUT: Many releases across several different catalogues, including Showcase Production Music (SPM), Instant Library Service, Instant Replay, Stereo, Trendsetter and The CAT. See also Sounds Of Broadcasting. Well over one hundred releases. STYLE: Jingles, standard industrials, novelties, some odd conceptual recordings for use in shopping malls, public announcements. SLEEVES: Each catalogue has its own distinctive style. The CAT is the only series to use illustration.

WORLD

Atmosfera Drammatica Romantica
Carlo Savina
Heavy drama and love. (JD)

HISTORY: Rome based organisation dating from the 1970s. Offshoot of Fonovideo. See also, Flam, Hard, Ring. OUTPUT: Catalogue numbers suggest fifteen LPs were produced. Difficult to locate. STYLE: Electronics, drama. MUSICIANS OF NOTE: Carlo Savina, Fabio Fabor. SLEEVES: Most have the 'world' graphic in different colourways. Some later photography.

SOME MUSICIANS' PSEUDONYMS

Alain Windus = Paul Bonneau
Alan Blackwell = Janko Nilovic
Alan Moorhouse = Alan Moor
Alex Alexander = Alessandro Alessandroni
A. L. Prévost = Raymond Guiot
Adam Best = Barry Stoller
Amedeo Forte = Amedeo Tommasi
Andy Loore = Janko Nilovic
Angel Oliver Pina = Carlo Rustichelli
Arawak = Benito Simoncini
Astra = Franco Battiato
Astemix = Remigio Ducros
Ataraxia = Mort Garson
Atmo = Amedeo Tommasi
Awake = Oronzo De Filippi
Bernie Powell = Berto Pisano
Bill Mayer = Janko Nilovic
Blue Marvin = Alberto Baldan Bembo
Bobbie Bennet = Cindy Wilson
Bob Deramont = Roberto Pregadio
Bob Mitchell = Augusto Martelli
Braen = Alessandro Alessandroni
Brother John = Johnny Cymbal
Bunny J. Browne = Johnny Hawksworth
Burt Rexon = Berto Pisano
Caldeo = Berto Pisano
Capricorn = Claudio Simonetti
Caravelli = Claude Vasori
Carlo El Rubio = Francois De Roubaix
Carl Rustic = Carlo Rustichelli
Catamo = Piero Umiliani
Cecil Leuter = Roger Roger
Charles Hanger = Carlo Savina
Chris Waxman = Klaus Wunderlich
Cisco El Rubio = Francois De Roubaix
Claude King = Claudio Simonetti
Cliff Johns = John Gale
Complesso Gisteri = Alessandro Alessandroni & Rino De Filippi
Dave Man = Roger Davy
Dan Savio = Ennio Morricone
David Perian = Paul Guiot
David Westcott = Yan Tregger
Dereales = Mario Migliardi
Donaway = Gianni Mazza
Donimak = Nico Fidenco
Doris Hays = Delia Derbyshire
Dwight St. John = David Snell
Early Freeman und sein Orchester = Mario Battaini
Ed De Joy = Franco Battiato
Emiliano Orti = Janko Nilovic
Ennio Morandi = Janko Nilovic
Eric Towren = Even De Tissot
Eric Framond = Camille Sauvage
Eric Swan = Roger Roger
E. Winkell = Coriolano Gori
Evirust = Carlo Rustichelli
Farlocco (means Fake in Italian) = Amedeo Tommasi / Stefano Torossi
Fotriafa = Stefano Torossi
Francis Berman = Armando Trovajoli
Francis D. Masion = Francesco De Masi
Francis Taylor = Franco Micalizzi
Frank Mason = Francesco De Masi
Frank Rothman = Frans Mijts
Gale Warning = Frances Day
Garth Watt-Roy = Leon Paul-Phillips
Gary Pacific = Wolfram Brunke
Gary Stevan = Stefano Torossi
Georges Teperino = Nino Nardini
Gias = Lucio Battisti
Girolamo Ugolini = Alessandro Alessandroni
Gisteri = Alessandro Alessandroni
Glen Somers = Reg Owen
G. Ployer = Gianfranco Plenizio
Graham Lane – Alan Parker
H. Caiage = Gerardo Iacoucci
Heat Exchange = Brian Bennett
Heinz Kube = Janko Nilovic
Herbana = Piero Umiliani
Hingross = Giorgio Ingrosso
H. Myrval = F. Bonfanti
H. Tical = Armando Sciascia
Ipcress = Stelvio Cipriani
Jack Melrose = Bernard Hulin
Jack Trombey = Jan Stoeckhart
Jacky Nodaro = Jacky Giordano
James Anderson = Gianni Ferrio
Jarrell = Amedeo Tommasi
Jay Richford = Giovanni Tommaso
Jean Pierre Valmére = Johnny Teupen
Jim Murphy = Carlo Rustichelli
J. Matthews = John Baker
J. Montevideo = Janko Nilovic
Joan Christian = Nora Orlandi
Joe Dynamo = Gianni Marchetti
Janos Lehar = John Leach
Johnny Sax = Gianni Bedori
John Servus = Gianni Marchetti
Jonefle = Piero Umiliani

Jonny Moggi = Piero Umiliani
Juniper = Guido & Maurizio De Angelis
Kasso = Claudio Simonetti
Kema = Alessandro Alessandroni
Lady Park = Gianni Ferrio
Larry Robbins = Gerhard Narholz
Latrudi = Massimo Catalano / Amedeo Tommasi
Laurence Vanay = Jacqueline Thibault
Laurie Driver = Reg Owen
Leo Petit = Michael Hington
Lee Mason = Pete Moore
Leo Flag = Bruno Nicolai
Leo Nichols = Ennio Morricone
Lesiman = Paolo Renosto
Li De la Russe = Delia Derbyshire
L'Ingegner Giovanni & Famiglia = Piero Umiliani
Litoz = Luigi Zito
Lucifer = Mort Garson
Luis Enríquez = Luis Enríque Bacalov
Malcolm Lockyer = Howard Shaw
Maneshandra Kansara = Big Jim Sullivan
Marco Melciori = Teisco
Marcus Griffin = Marcello Giombini
Michel Trenne / M. Trenne = Klaus Weiss
Milton Hunter = Harry Rabinowitz
Milt Rotterdam = Sam Sklair
Mirageman = Giovanni Fenati
Mitridate = Giampiero Boneschi
Moggi = Piero Umiliani
Mustang = Elvio Monti
M. Zalla = Piero Umiliani
Narassa = Sandro Brugnolini / Amedeo Tommasi
Nikki St. George = Brian Hodgson
Ninety = Gian Piero Reverberi
Nuan = Antonello Vannucchi
Oliver Onions = Guido & Maurizio De Angelis
Otto Sieben = Gerhard Narholz
Oscar Lindok = Giacomo Dell'Orso
Pantros = Armando Sciascia
Paul Clemente = Bruno Nicolai
Paul Gerard = Dennis Farnon
Paul Kass = Johnny Hawksworth
Paul Nero = Klaus Doldinger
Pelleus = Elvio Monti
Peter Bonello = Nino Nardini
Peter Covent = Carlos Diernhammer
Peter Milray = Jan Stoeckhart
Peter O'Milian = Piero Umiliani
Peter Pietra = Piero Umiliani
Peter Reno = Clifford Twemlow
Peymont = Luigi Malatesta / Egisto Macchi
Philippe Gray = Janko Nilovic
Piero Morgan = Piero Piccioni
Piet van Meren = Pete Moore
Plakoti = Gianni Ferrio
Pluto Kennedy = Marcello Giombini
Pontiak = Francesco Guccini
Proluton = Giacomo Dell'Orso
Raiword = Piero Umiliani
Raskovich = Giuliano Sorgini
Richard Ira Silver = Sante Maria Romitelli
Richard Neve = Keith Mansfield
Rich Hero = Richard Gibbons
Rimauri = Teisco
Robin Artus = Roger Limb
Roger Higgins = Riz Ortolani
Romano Full = Romano Mussolini
Roman Vatro = Armando Trovajoli
Rovi = Piero Umiliani
Ruscigan = Piero Umiliani
Sammy Burdson = Gerhard Narholz
Santany = Romolo Grano
Scoen = Enzo Scoppa
Sitimo = Piero Umiliani
Sordini = Giuliano Sorgini
Steve Powder / Power = Stelvio Cipriani
Ted Atking = Jack Arel
The Duke of Burlington = Mario Battaini
The Texas Travellers = Janko Nilovic
The Trendsetters = James Clarke
Tony Rallo = Francois De Roubaix
Tony Tape = Gerhard Narholz
Transformers L.T.D. = Alessandro Alessandroni & others or Giacomo Dell'Orso
Tusco = Piero Umiliani
Vasco = Stefano Torossi
Virginie Morgan = Michel Ramos
Walter Warren = James De Wolfe
Walter Ritz | Walt Ritz = Walter Rizzati
Walt Rockman = Gerhard Narholz
Werter Pierazzuoli = Egisto Macchi
William Gum Boot = JP Decerf
William Parrish = Alan Hawkshaw
William Stanray = Michael Hington
Willie Pat Roon = Lino Patruno
Zalla = Piero Umiliani
Zanagoria = Giorgio Carnini
Zibelius = Mario Molino

Just some of the labels we sadly didn't have room for, but should be mentioned and are worth exploring:

Abramo Allione
Air Force
Airplane
Airwaves
Alto Livello
Alto Music
Arlecchino
Atmosphere
Atoll
Audial
Auessi Records
Aureus
Bam
BBB Records
Bella Brace
Black
Bridget Music
Capriccio
Cardium
Carillo
CBS Songs
Chandos
Chic
Ciak
C.I.C.
City
Comprehensive
Conny
Count Records
Cuban Records
D.I. Music
Dardo Records
Dischi Ricordi
Disc Litanie
Dreyfus
Easy Records Italiana
Edition Panther And Co
Ellecci
Emergency
E.M.R.
Europhon
Folkmusic
Fono Film
Gaumont Musique
Globevision
Herkules
Hitfor
Horse Shoe
Inmus
KTS (Kuhn Teupen Sounds)
Le Monde / LMR
LGO Music
Magic Record
Magma
Master Plus
Maximus
Melodie
MFA (South Africa)
Network
NFL Music Library
Nuovo Repetorio Editoriale
Original Disc
Orix
Paloma Records
Pema
Poker
Raphaele
Rodenstein
SAAR Library
Sab Mag
Sam Fox
Santanna Records
Seeburg Music Library
SEL
Shepherds Bush
Sibilla
Sign
Sir Winston
Small Frog
Soundways
Spring
Spectrum
Standard Sound Production
Star Track
Studio One
Style
Tamo
Tapes Sound
Team
Telerecord
Time
TM Productions
Traks
Travel Music
Trend
Try
Twins
Union
Valentino
Weekend

Afterword

I think it was Mr Fraser Moss who first turned me on to library records, back when he was introducing me to all manner of arcane syncopated electronics. I soon became lost in a world of abstract percussion by delirious Frenchmen and strange mellifluous soundtracks, scored and played for non-existent adverts in Wardour Street studios.

To me it feels like a bizarre parallel world, a reflection of the styles and tropes of five hundred years of popular music. Or like a journey through the mirror, in a sequence from a seventies Hammer film, to a place where nobody knows how to distinguish between the genres: rock, jazz, pop, avant-garde, electronic, baroque, folk...

A sidereal arena to the contemporary world of pop chart positionings.

They're like concept albums. The concept is an abstract idea that's already in place and the musicians – various jazznik session musos and visionaries with effects boxes – have to interpret it. Industry in motion, landscape, contemporary baroque, anguish and mystery. I like the themes and the track descriptions – neutral underscore; nervous energy; uneasy, sparse, thick chords, disturbed – as above with spiky interjections.

The name Library has a resonance of archives, dusty volumes, musty rooms containing filed memories and ideas. And searching for these records you sometimes feel like a character in an H.P. Lovecraft story, discovering arcane tomes in dusty backrooms and Parisian flea markets. For me its always been about the strange atmospheres etched into the vinyl – not breakbeats or the more obvious DJ sample fodder.

And perfectly reflecting all of this are the sleeves. Beguiling abstractions and collages, wonky typography, a bad but good design free for all, unfettered by commercial constraints (well, they're for commercial use but not in the record shop / chart market place). There are great series of sleeves, simple pop art geometry and colour coding that demands that you hunt down every one. The truly bizarre collages on some, bordering on outsider art, fit perfectly with the angular, disjointed moods of the music – as if the musicians and designer are working from the same brief.

The sleeves have been a huge influence on me, for their brash pop surrealism (rivaled only by Polish film posters), their subtle but clunky type and their simple multiple sleeves with colour changes.

Working with bands like Stereolab and Broadcast inspires a way of designing which represents the album, its colours, tone and vision. Packaging that's wrapped inside the music.

Julian House

Jonny Trunk started Trunk Records in 1995. The first release was the library compilation *The Super Sounds Of Bosworth*. Still obsessed by library and film music, Trunk continues to issue rare lost recordings, DJs internationally, broadcasts through the medium of television and radio and sources beautiful and often strange music for television and film.

This book has been a dream for many years, and has only been made possible thanks to FUEL and the record collections of the fellow library fanatics I've met over the last two decades. JT

THE CONTRIBUTORS

Cherrystones (C) Recording artist, compiler and remarkably dark DJ.
Jerry Dammers (JD) Former 'Special'.
Jazzman Gerald (JG) The man behind Jazzman Records.
Chris Gibbons (CG) Mondo DJ, educator, multi-media artist.
Simon Gitter (SG) Trusty librarian and archivist.
Martin Green (MG) DJ to the stars.
Ben Horner (BH) Artist and painter.
Julian House (JH) Graphic designer and co-owner of Ghost Box.
Intoxica! (I) Legendary vintage record store on Portobello Road, London.
James Karminsky (JK) Part One of the Karminsky Experience.
Martin Karminsky (MK) Part Two of the Karminsky Experience.
Joel Martin (JM) Early library entrepreneur, DJ and collector.
Fraser Moss (FM) Head designer at You Must Create.
Sermad (S) Obsessive library fiend.
James Pianta (JP) Archivist, founder of Votary, Roundtable & Dual Planet.
Justin Spear (JS) DJ, collector, writer and occasional broadcaster.
Steve Stasis (SS) Collector turned masseuse.
Jonny Trunk (JT)
John Tye (LO) Head of Lo Recordings.
Luke Vibert (LV) International DJ, artist and collector.
Patrick Whitaker (PW) aka 'The Quadfather', film fashion designer.
Simon White (SW) Mid-century modernist.

Very special thanks to Paul Sandell at KPM /EMI. Further thanks must go to the following: Warren De Wolfe and Steve Rosie at De Wolfe Music, John Wraight at Bucks Music, Howard Friend at Bosworths, Godsey for research on all his (C) LPs, Richard Dawson at Happy Retouching, and all the adventurous musical explorers who have kept the sound of old library music alive and very well indeed.

NOTE: This book catalogues music of the 1960s, 1970s and 1980s. Some of the record labels are still in existence today and it must be understood that our musical style information does not take into consideration contemporary recordings.

'Output' refers to the number of titles the label issued. Where possible exact LP issue numbers are used, otherwise estimates have been given.